III.) Calumet Club (Chicago

Early Chicago

reception to the settlers of Chicago prior to 1840, by the Calumet Club, of Chicago, Tuesday evening, May 27, 1879

III.) Calumet Club (Chicago

Early Chicago
reception to the settlers of Chicago prior to 1840, by the Calumet Club, of Chicago, Tuesday evening, May 27, 1879

ISBN/EAN: 9783337414405

Printed in Europe, USA, Canada, Australia, Japan

Cover: Foto ©Andreas Hilbeck / pixelio.de

More available books at **www.hansebooks.com**

Early Chicago.

RECEPTION

TO THE

SETTLERS OF CHICAGO

PRIOR TO 1840,

BY

THE CALUMET CLUB,

OF CHICAGO,

TUESDAY EVENING, MAY 27, 1879.

CHICAGO:
THE CALUMET CLUB,
MICHIGAN AVENUE AND EIGHTEENTH STREET.
1879.

CONTENTS.

	PAGE.
Officers and members of THE CALUMET CLUB,	5
Origin of the Reception,	9
Record of Old Settlers who were invited,	11
The Reception,	23
Prayer of Rev. STEPHEN R. BEGGS,	23
Speech of Rev. STEPHEN R. BEGGS,	24
Address of welcome, by Gen. HENRY STRONG,	26
Speech of Ex-Chief-Justice JOHN DEAN CATON,	35
Speech of Judge HENRY W. BLODGETT,	43
Speech of Judge JAMES GRANT,	45
Speech of Hon. JOHN WENTWORTH,	45
Speech of Judge GRANT GOODRICH,	62
Speech of Hon. J. YOUNG SCAMMON,	65
Speech of Hon. WM. BROSS,	70
Tables showing places of birth, years of arrival, and ages of those who attended and signed the Register,	72
Appendix: Letter from JOHN WATKINS,	73
Letter from NORMAN K. TOWNER,	74
Letter from Rev. FLAVEL BASCOM,	76
Letter from Maj-Gen. DAVID HUNTER,	76
Letter from Judge EBENEZER PECK,	77
Letter from Rev. JEREMIAH PORTER,	77
Names of those from whom brief letters of regret were received,	78
Extract from Chicago Tribune,	79
Extract from Chicago Evening Journal,	81
Register of Old Settlers,	83

Officers and Members

PRESIDENT,
ANSON STAGER.

VICE-PRESIDENT,
CHARLES J. BARNES.

SECRETARY AND TREASURER,
FREDERICK B. TUTTLE.

DIRECTORS:

CHARLES J. BARNES, JAMES B. GOODMAN,
WATSON F. BLAIR, EDSON KEITH,
WILLIAM CHISHOLM, ROBERT L. PERRY,
CHARLES W. DREW, ANSON STAGER,
AUGUSTUS N. EDDY, FREDERICK B. TUTTLE,
A. G. VAN SCHAICK,

MEMBERS:

ADSIT, JAMES M., Jr. ASAY, J. F.
ALDRICH, WILLIAM ASHWELL, W. C.
ALEXANDER, G. M. AVERILL, A. J.
ALLERTON, SAML. W. AYERS, ENOS
ANDERSON, T. W. BACON, HENRY M.
ANDREWS, JOSEPH H. BACON, ROSWELL B.
ANGELL, WM. A. BAKER, WM. T.
ARMOUR, GEO. A. BAKER, W. VINCENT
ARMOUR, JOSEPH F. BALCOM, URI
ASAY, E. G. BALLARD, D. P.

Barnes, Chas. J.
Barrett, O. W.
Bartlett, A. C.
Bartlett, Chas. S.
Bigelow, A. A.
Billings, Chas. A.
Billings, H. F.
Birch, Hugh T.
Bishop, Henry W.
Blackstone, T. B.
Blair, Chauncey B.
Blair, Chauncey J.
Blair, Watson F.
Borland, J. J.
Briggs, Clinton
Brown, Andrew
Brown, J. M.
Bryant, J. Ogden
Buckingham, C.
Burnham, D. H.
Byford, Henry T.
Campbell, Augustus S.
Campbell, B. H., Jr.
Carver, W. S.
Cassidy, J. A.
Caton, Arthur J.
Chisholm, Wm.
Chumasero, John T.
Clark, John M.
Clark, Stewart
Cleaveland, Jas. O.
Cobb, Calvin
Cobb, Silas B.
Coburn, Chas. E.
Coburn, Lewis L.

Coleman, Joseph G.
Collier, Clinton
Comes, Charles W.
Connell, Chas. J.
Cooper, E. M.
Corwith, Gurden
Corwith, Henry
Corwith, Nathan
Counselman, Chas.
Cowles, Alfred
Cox, R. W.
Crane, Albert
Crane, Charles A.
Crerar, John
Culbertson, C. M., Jr.
Critchell, R. S.
Derby, W. M.
Dewey, A. A.
Doane, J. W.
Dodge, Geo. E. P.
Drake, John B.
Drew, Charles W.
Dwight, J. H.
Eddy, Augustus N.
Fairbank, N. K.
Fargo, Charles
Fauntleroy, T. S.
Field, Marshall
Fisher, Fred. P.
Fleetwood, Chas.
Fleetwood, Stanley
Fleming, Robert H.
Fuller, Geo. W.
Fuller, Wm. A.
Gage, Albert S.

LIST OF MEMBERS.

Gardner, C. S.
Getchell, E. F.
Glover, Samuel J.
Goodman, Jas. B.
Goodwin, Jonathan
Gore, George P.
Gorton, Anson
Gould, M. B.
Grannis, W. C. D.
Gray, Franklin D.
Grey, Wm. L.
Hall, Amos T.
Hackney, H. C.
Hackney, John J.
Hall, Wm. S.
Hamill, Chas. D.
Hamill, Ernest A.
Hanford, P. C.
Hardin, S. H.
Haskell, Fred. T.
Heaton, E. S.
Henderson, E. F.
Henry, R. L.
Hibbard, Wm. G.
Hodges, L.
Holliday, John M.
Hoyne, F. G.
Hoyne, T. M.
Hughes, John B.
Hutchins, C. S.
Hyman, R. W., Jr.
Isham, Henry P.
Jansen, E. L.
Jenkins, T. R.
Johnston, Wm. J.

Jones, S. J.
Judah, Noble B.
Keep, Albert
Keep, Chauncey
Keep, Fred. A.
Keep, Henry
Keith, Edson
Keith, O. R.
Kelley, David
Kellogg, A. N.
Kimball, C. Fred.
Kimball, C. P.
Kimball, Mark
Kimball, W. W.
Kimbark, S. D.
Kirkpatrick, W. E.
Knickerbocker, Joshua C.
Knight, W. S.
Lay, A. Tracy
Law, Robert
Leiter, Levi Z.
Lester, John T.
Logan, John A.
Loomis, John Mason
Ludington, Nelson
May, Edward
Marshall, Geo. E.
McClelland, H. W.
Miller, DeLaskie
Miller, R. B.
Mitchell, John J.
Morley, E. W.
Morse, T. E.
Oakley, J. W.
Ogden, J. W.

OLMSTEAD, EDWARD
OTIS, GEO. L.
OTIS, JOS. E.
OTIS, PHILO A.
OTIS, X. L.
PACKARD, EDWARD A.
PAGE, WM. R.
PEACOCK, C. D.
PECK, CLARENCE I.
PECK, FERD. W.
PECK, JOHN L.
PERRY, R. L.
PHELPS, ERSKINE M.
POWELL, SAMUEL
PULLMAN, GEO. M.
QUICK, JOHN H. S.
RALSTON, R. W.
ROCKWELL, A. L.
ROE, JOHN
ROGERS, JOHN G.
ROOT, JOHN W.
SARD, WM. H.
SAWYER, E. T.
SCHNEIDER, GEO.
SEEBERGER, A. F.
SEEBERGER, C. D.
SHAY, M. D.
SHEPARD, J. H.
SHERIDAN, P. H.
SHIPMAN, DANIEL B.
SKEELE, J. H.
SMITH, BYRON L.
SMITH, FRED. L.

STAGER, ANSON
STEARNS, M. C.
STEVENS, GEORGE E.
STONE, JOSEPH A.
STORRS, EMORY A.
STRONG, HENRY
TENNEY, D. K.
THACHER, J. M.
THOMPSON, JOHN L.
TUCKER, W. F., Jr.
TUTTLE, FREDERICK
TUTTLE, FREDERICK B.
VAIL, H. S.
VAN SCHAACK, PETER
VAN SCHAICK, A. G.
WALKER, WM. B.
WALTER, JOEL C.
WATSON, WM., Jr.
WELLS, M. D.
WENTWORTH, MOSES J.
WETMORE, C. L.
WHEATON, GEO. D.
WHEELER, C. T.
WHEELER, EZRA J.
WHEELER, H. N.
WHITNEY, J. C.
WIGHT, THOMAS
WILBOR, PHILO A
WILLIAMS, ABRAM
WILLIAMS, CLIFFORD
WILLIAMS, NORMAN
WILSON, HUGH R.
WOODRUFF, CHAS. W.

July 21st, 1879.

ORIGIN OF THE RECEPTION.

AT the first annual meeting of THE CALUMET CLUB, held on the 5th of May, 1879, it was. on motion of Mr. JOEL C. WALTER, seconded by Mr. CHARLES S. HUTCHINGS,

Resolved, That THE CALUMET CLUB will give a Reception to the "Old Settlers" who resided in Chicago prior to the year 1840.

At a special meeting of the Board of Directors of THE CALUMET CLUB, held on the 10th day of May, 1879, it was, on motion of Mr. AUGUSTUS N. EDDY, seconded by Mr. WM. CHISHOLM,

Resolved, That a committee of three to consist of the Vice-President—Mr. CHARLES J. BARNES, the Secretary—Mr. FREDERICK B. TUTTLE, and Mr. A. G. VAN SCHAICK, be and is hereby appointed with power to act, by this Board, to confer with Messrs. SILAS B. COBB, FRANKLIN D. GRAY, MARK KIMBALL, JAS. H. REES, MARCUS C. STEARNS, FREDERICK TUTTLE, and JOEL C. WALTER, and to make all necessary arrangements for the Reception to be given to the "Old Settlers" of Chicago.

RECORD OF OLD SETTLERS,

NOW LIVING,

WHO CAME TO CHICAGO PRIOR TO 1840,

AND WERE

INVITED TO THE RECEPTION OF THE CALUMET CLUB,
TUESDAY, MAY 27TH, 1879,

COMPILED BY

THE OLD SETTLERS COMMITTEE:

SILAS B. COBB,

MARK KIMBALL,   MARCUS C. STEARNS,   FRANKLIN D. GRAY,
JAMES H. REES,   FREDERICK TUTTLE,   JOEL C. WALTER.

The Committee, being obliged to compile this Record principally from memory, may have inadvertently ommitted the names of some persons still living.

Adams, Charles,	Norwalk, Conn.
Adams, Joseph,	South Evanston, Ill.
Adams, William H.	454 Wabash Ave., Chicago.
Adsit, James M.	947 Prairie Ave., Chicago.
Allen, Edward R.	Aurora, Ill.
Allen, Thomas,	Glencoe, Ill.
Allison, Thomas,	West Northfield, Ill.
Arnold, Isaac N.	104 Pine Street, Chicago.
Bailey, Amos,	San Jose, Cal.
Bailey, Bennett,	301 Fulton Street, Chicago.
Baker, Franklin,	30 Oakwood Boulevard, Chicago.
Baldwin, W. A.	265½ Illinois Street, Chicago.
Balestier, Joseph N.	Brattleboro, Vermont.
Balsley, John,	301 W. Congress St., Chicago.
Barnes, R. B.	Jefferson, Ill.
Bascom, Flavel,	Hinsdale, Ill.

Batchelor, Ezra, — Milwaukee, Wis.
Bates, John, — 254 State St., Chicago.
Baumgarten, Chris. — Freeport, Ill.
Baumgarten, John, — Freeport, Ill.
Beach, James S. — 31 Walnut St., Chicago.
Beaubien, Mark, — Newark, Kendall Co., Ill.
Beaubien, Medore B. — Silver Lake, Kan.
Beecher, Jerome, — 241 Michigan Ave., Chicago.
Beggs, Stephen R. — Plainfield, Ill.
Berdel, Nicholas, — Cor. 59th and State Sts., Chicago.
Berg, Anton, — 307 5th Ave., Chicago.
Bishop, James, E. — Denver, Col.
Black, Francis, — Hampton, Ill.
Blake, E. Sanford, — Waseca, Minn.
Blackman, Edwin, — Room 11, 70 LaSalle St., Chicago.
Blake, L. S. — Racine, Wis.
Blasy, Barnhard, — Chicago.
Blodgett, H. W. — Waukegan, Ill.
Boone, L. D. — 665 Michigan Ave., Chicago.
Botsford, J. K. — 613 Michigan Ave., Chicago.
Botsford, Moss, — Grant Park, Ill.
Bowen, Erastus S. — City Hall, Chicago.
Boyer, V. A. — 233 N. Wells St., Chicago.
Bradley, A. F. — Jefferson, Cook Co., Ill.
Bradley, Timothy M. — Room 11, 157 LaSalle St., Chicago.
Bradwell, J. B. — Chicago.
Bridges, T. B. — Oak Park, Ill.
Brooks, Henry, — Hyde Park, Ill.
Brooks, Joshua, — Galena, Ill.
Brooks, Saml. M. — San Francisco, Cal.
Brown, Andrew J. — Evanston, Ill.
Brown, Lemuel, — Iowa.
Brown, Nathaniel J. — Lemont, Ill.
Brown, W. H. — 15 N. Morgan St., Chicago.
Bryan, F. A. — No. 1 Bryan Place, Chicago.

Burley, A. G.	636 Indiana Ave., Chicago.
Burley, A. H.	254 Dearborn Ave., Chicago.
Burley, Charles,	Exeter, N. H.
Butler, John H.	Jefferson, Ill.
Campbell, James,	296 Calumet Ave., Chicago.
Canda, Florimond,	Beau Rivage, Chicago.
Carpenter, A. E.	Aurora, Ill.
Carpenter, Philo,	57 Ashland Ave., Chicago.
Carroll, Edward,	Chicago.
Carter, T. B.	20th Street, Chicago.
Caton, J. D.	Ottawa, Ill.
Chacksfield, Geo.	208 Fulton Street, Chicago.
Chamberlin, Rev. J. S.	Robin's Nest, Ill.
Church, W. L.	Kenwood, Ill.
Clark, John L.	208 Michigan Ave., Chicago.
Clark, L. J.	188 Madison Street, Chicago.
Clark, Norman,	Racine, Wis.
Clarke, A. F.	Marietta, Ga.
Clarke, Henry W.	92 Washington Street, Chicago.
Clarke, Samuel C.	Marietta, Ga.
Cleaver, Charles,	Ellis Ave., near 42nd St., Chicago.
Cleaver, Edward C.	1733 Indiana Ave., Chicago.
Coldwell, Archibald,	Kershena, Wis.
Cobb, S. B.	S.-W. cor. Prairie Ave. & 21st St.
Cook, Isaac,	St. Louis, Mo.
Cook, Thomas,	Cass Precinct, Dupage Co., Ill.
Corrigan, William,	N.-W. cor. State & 18th Sts.
Couch, James,	Tremont House, Chicago.
Crocker, Hans,	Milwaukee, Wis.
Davlin, John,	Waukegan, Ill.
Davidson, O.	Elgin, Ill.
Densmore, E. W.	1064 Indiana Ave., Chicago.
Dewey, D. S.	Monticello, Iowa.
DeWolf, Calvin,	179 Vincennes Ave., Chicago.
Dexter, A. A.	Union Stock Yards.

14 CALUMET CLUB.

Dickey, Hugh T.	Newport, R. I.
Dickinson, Augustus,	1106 Indiana Ave., Chicago.
Dodge, Martin,	Montague, Michigan.
Dodge, Usual S.	Plymouth, Indiana.
Dodson, C. B.	Geneva, Ill.
Doty, Theodorus,	273 30th Street, Chicago.
Drummond, Thomas,	Winfield, Dupage Co., Ill.
Duck, Charles H.	Chicago.
Dyer, George R.	Joliet, Ill.
Edgell, Stephen M.	St. Louis, Mo.
Egan, W. M.	Chicago.
Eldridge, J. W.	Grand Pacific Hotel, Chicago.
Ellis, Joel,	62 W. Jackson Street, Chicago.
Elliott, James F. D.	Matteson, Will Co., Ill.
Ellithorpe, A. C.	144 S. Ashland Ave., Chicago.
Fake, Henry,	Chicago.
Fergus, Robert,	244 Illinois Street, Chicago.
Filer, Alanson,	Racine, Wis.
Flood, Peter F.	93 S. Sangamon Street, Chicago.
Follansbee, Charles,	1027 Wabash Ave., Chicago.
Freeman, Robert,	Naperville, Ill.
Freer, L. C. Paine,	247 Michigan Ave., Chicago.
Fullerton, A. N.	Evanston, Ill.
Gage, Jared,	Wynetka, Ill.
Gage, John,	Wynetka, Ill.
Gale, Abram,	Galewood, Ill.
Gale, Stephen, F.	45 S. Peoria Street, Chicago.
Gates, P. W.	52 S. Canal Street, Chicago.
Germaine, George H.	11 Boston Ave., Chicago.
Gilbert, Samuel H.	333 Walnut Street, Chicago.
Goodrich, Grant,	40 Rush Street, Chicago.
Goodrich, T. W.	Milwaukee, Wis.
Goold, Nathaniel,	248 State Street, Chicago.
Graff, Peter,	42 Curtiss Street, Chicago.
Granger, Elihu,	Kaneville, Ill.

Grannis, Amos,	1112 Indiana Ave., Chicago.
Grannis, S. W.	Park Ridge, Ill.
Grant, James,	Davenport, Iowa.
Gray, Charles M.	1171 Wabash Ave., Chicago.
Gray, Franklin D.	333 Michigan Ave., Chicago.
Gray, George M.	Grand Pacific Hotel, Chicago.
Gray, John,	Jefferson, Ill.
Gray, Joseph H.	Hyde Park, Ill.
Gray, W. B. H.	Lake Ave., near 38th St., Chicago.
Graves, Henry,	Cottage Grove Ave., near 33rd St.
Greene, Russell,	
Gurnee, Walter S.	New York City.
Hackett, John,	Beloit, Wis.
Haddock, E. H.	Cor. Mich. Ave. & 30th St., Chicago.
Haines, E. M.	78 5th Ave., Chicago.
Haines, John C.	185 S. Sangamon Street, Chicago.
Hall, Benjamin,	Wheaton, Ill.
Hallam, Rev. Isaac W.	New Caanan, Conn.
Hamilton, P. D.	Chicago.
Hanchett, John L.	5 Hubbard Court, Chicago.
Harmon, Isaac D.	309 30th Street, Chicago.
Harmon, Isaac N.	52 River Street, Chicago.
Harmon, E. R.	52 River Street, Chicago.
Harrington, A. M.	Geneva, Ill.
Harrington, James C.	Geneva, Ill.
Hastings, Hiram,	20 Adams Street, Chicago.
Hawley, John S.	Aurora, Ill.
Heald, Hamilton,	Oak Ridge, Ill.
Hickling, William,	104 Calumet Ave., Chicago.
Higgins, Van H.	Kenwood, Ill.
Hilliard, Lorin P.	Chicago.
Hitchcock, Rev. Luke,	Cincinnati, Ohio.
Hoard, Samuel,	205 Morgan Street, Chicago.
Holden, Charles N.	542 W. Monroe Street, Chicago.
Horton, D.	447 Michigan Ave., Chicago.

16   CALUMET CLUB.

Howe, F. A.	Wabash Ave., Chicago.
Hoyne, Thomas,	88 LaSalle Street, Chicago.
Hubbard, G. S.	243 White Street, Chicago.
Hubbard, Thomas H.	Bank of Commerce, New York.
Hugunin, James R.	Chicago.
Hugunin, L. C.	Cor. Blue Island Ave. & 16th St.
Humphreys, A. A.	Washington, D. C.
Hunter, David,	Washington, D. C.
Hunter, George W.	Willmette, Ill.
Huntington, Alonzo,	94 Dearborn Street, Chicago.
Huntoon, George M.	Evanston, Ill.
Jones, Fernando,	Chicago.
Jones, N. A.	811 Wabash Ave., Chicago.
Kehoe, Michael,	390 W. Twelfth Street, Chicago.
Kennicott, Jonathan A.	Kenwood, Ill.
Kennicott, Joseph E.	Dunton, Ill.
Kettlestring, Joseph,	Oak Park, Ill.
Kimball, Harlow,	Oakland, California.
Kimball, Mark,	984 Prairie Ave., Chicago.
Kimball, Walter,	930 Indiana Ave., Chicago.
Kimball, Martin N.	Jefferson, Ill.
King, Tuthil,	831 Michigan Ave., Chicago.
Knickerbocker, H. W.	Naperville, Ill.
Knight, Darius	939 Indiana Ave., Chicago,
Kuhl, John,	Cor. Chicago & Ashland Aves.
Laflin, George H.	585 Michigan Ave., Chicago.
Laflin, Mathew,	6 Park Row, Chicago.
Lane, Elisha B.	321 W. Madison Street, Chicago.
Lane, George W.	Morris, Ill.
Larrabee, William M.	91 Adams Street, Chicago.
Lathrop, Samuel,	Bristol, Ill.
Leavenworth, J. H.	Milwaukee, Wis.
Lind, Sylvester,	Lake Forest, Ill.
Lock, William,	475 Michigan Ave., Chicago.
Loomis, Henry,	Burlington, Vermont.

Loomis, H. G.	Naperville, Ill.
Magill, Julian,	Paris, France.
Maher, Hugh,	Michigan Ave. & 51st St., Chicago.
Malony, Mathew S.	Belvidere, Ill.
Manierre, Edward,	Chicago.
Markoe, Hartman,	New York City.
Marshall, James A.	Chicago.
Marsh, Sylvester,	
McCarthy, Owen,	192 S. Sangamon Street, Chicago.
McClure, Josiah E.	684 Michigan Ave., Chicago.
McDonnell, Charles,	Chicago.
McDaniel, Alexander,	Willmette, Ill.
McKee, David,	Aurora, Ill.
McIntosh, David,	
Metz, Christopher,	107 22nd Street, Chicago.
Milliken, Isaac L.	Monee, Will Co., Ill.
Mills, John R.	1120 Michigan Ave., Chicago.
Miltimore, Ira,	Janesville, Wis.
Morgan, P. R.	Chicago.
Moore, Robert,	Chicago.
Morris, Buckner S.	Lytle, N. E. cor. W. Taylor St.
Morrison, Daniel,	Chicago.
Morrison, Ephraim,	172 W. Monroe Street, Chicago.
Morrison, Ezekiel,	125 Clark Street, Chicago.
Murphy, James K.	152 LaSalle Street, Chicago.
Murray, R. N.	Naperville, Ill.
Myrick, Willard F.	142 Vernon Ave., Chicago.
Nichols, Luther,	106 S. Peoria Street, Chicago.
Noble, John,	743 Sedgwick Street, Chicago.
Norton, Nelson R.	Alden, Minnesota.
Ogden, Mahlon D.	Elmhurst, Ill.
Osborn, Andrew L.	La Porte, Indiana.
Osborn, William,	Chicago.
Page, Peter,	661 Michigan Ave., Chicago.
Pardee, Theron,	815 W. Washington St., Chicago.

Parker, John,	Hinsdale, Ill.
Parker, Thomas L.	
Peacock, Elijah,	98 State Street, Chicago.
Peacock, Joseph,	196 S. Peoria Street, Chicago.
Peck, Ebenezer,	15 Walton Place, Chicago.
Peters, George,	New York City.
Pitkin, Nathaniel,	Wis.
Pierce, Asahel.	Mich. Ave., N.-W. cor. 40th St.
Pierce, Smith D.	Belmont, Iowa.
Plum, William B.	Aurora, Ill.
Pool, Captain J. W.	149 W. Washington St., Chicago.
Porter, Hibbard,	N.-W. cor. Mich. Ave. & 33rd St.
Porter, Rev. Jeremiah,	Fort D. A. Russell, Wy. T.
Porter, Rev. J. G.	
Prindeville, John,	92 LaSalle Street, Chicago.
Prindeville, Redmond,	213 Elm Street, Chicago.
Rand, Socrates,	161 N. Carpenter Street, Chicago.
Raymond, B. W.	Calumet Ave. & 23rd St., Chicago.
Rees, James H.	Chicago.
Reis, John M.	
Reis, Jacob,	
Reis, John P.	
Rexford, Norman,	Blue Island, Ill.
Rexford, Stephen,	Blue Island, Ill.
Richards, J. J.	Evanston, Ill.
Rogers, Edward K.	359 Ontario Street, Chicago.
Root, J. S.	Buffalo, New York.
Rue, John C.	131 S. Jefferson Street, Chicago.
Rumsey, George F.	70 LaSalle Street, Chicago.
Rumsey, Julien S.	70 LaSalle Street, Chicago.
Ryan, E. G.	Madison, Wis.
Saltonstall, F. G.	128 LaSalle Street, Chicago.
Satterlee, M. L.	830 Michigan Ave., Chicago.
Sawyer, Nathaniel,	Lake Forest, Ill.
Sawyer, Sidney,	301 Ontario Street, Chicago.

Scammon, J. Y.	Hyde Park, Ill.
Scott, Willard,	Naperville, Ill.
Scott, Willis,	199 W. Washington St., Chicago.
Scoville, William H.	Chicago.
Shapley, Morgan L.	Meridian, Bosque Co., Texas.
Sherman, A. S.	Waukegan, Ill.
Sherman, Ezra L.	Riverside, Ill.
Sherman, Frank T.	1253 Indiana Ave., Chicago.
Sherman, J. S.	East Northfield, Ill.
Sherman, O.	284 Wabash Ave., Chicago.
Skinner, Mark,	154 Lake Street, Chicago.
Smith, D. S.	402 Michigan Ave., Chicago.
Smith, Elijah,	215 37th Street, Chicago.
Smith, George,	Aberdeen, Scotland.
Smith, Joseph F.	83 Warren Ave., Chicago.
Snowhook, W. B.	61 LaSalle Street, Chicago.
Sollett, John,	157 S. Jefferson Street, Chicago.
Soules, Rufus,	Waukegan, Ill.
Spaulding, S. F.	
Speer, Isaac,	Randolph St., S.-W. cor. 5th Ave.
Stanton, D. D.	Norwich, Conn.
Stearns, Marcus C.	475 Wabash Ave., Chicago.
Steele, J. W.	42 Rush Street, Chicago.
Stevens, Thomas H.	U. S. Navy, Erie, Pa.
Stewart, Hart L.	1175 Prairie Ave., Chicago.
Stone, Lewis W.	Mich. Ave. & 43rd St., Chicago.
Stow, H. M.	Chicago.
Stow, W. H.	Chicago.
Strail, Milo,	Brooklyn, New York.
Sturtevant, A. D.	180 Warren Ave., Chicago.
Surdam, S. J.	Chicago.
Sweeney, John,	Chicago.
Swift, R. K.	
Talcott, E. B.	606 Wabash Ave., Chicago.
Taylor, A. D.	398 W. Taylor Street, Chicago.

Taylor, E. D.	Chicago.
Taylor, Ezra,	Chicago.
Taylor, Reuben,	714 W. Washington St., Chicago.
Taylor, William H.	Brookline, Mass.
Temple, Peter,	Lexington, Mo.
Toner, John,	
Towner, N. K.	Ypsilanti, Michigan.
Tripp, Robinson,	683 Wabash Ave., Chicago.
Turner, John,	Ravenswood, Ill.
Turner, John M.	1263 Indiana Ave., Chicago.
Turner, Leighton,	Evanston, Ill.
Tuttle, Frederick,	721 Michigan Ave., Chicago.
Tuttle, Lucius G.	998 Wabash Ave.,[died July 15, '79
Underwood, John M.	1321 State Street, Chicago.
Vail, Walter,	Newburgh, New York.
Vallette, Henry F.	Wheaton, Ill.
Vandercook, Charles R.	1321 State Street, Chicago.
Van Nortwick, John,	Batavia, Ill.
Van Osdel, John M.	41 Clark Street, Chicago.
Wadhams, Carlton,	South Bend, Indiana.
Wadhams, Seth,	Elmhurst, Ill.
Wadsworth, E. S.	393 Dearborn Street, Chicago.
Wadsworth, Julius,	New York City.
Waite, George W.	Hyde Park, Ill.
Walter, Joel C.	619 Michigan Ave., Chicago.
Walton, N. C.	
Warner, Seth P.	Austin, Cook Co., Ill.
Warner, Spencer,	17 Bryan Block, Chicago.
Waters, Benjamin,	
Watkins, John,	Joliet, Ill.
Wentworth, John,	Sherman House, Chicago.
Whitehead, Rev. Henry,	73 Randolph Street, Chicago.
Wicker, Charles G.	Yankton, Dakota Territory.
Wicker, Joel H.	St. Joseph, Michigan,

Wilcox, S. N.	
Wilde, George W.	Belvidere, Ill.
Willard, A. J.	79 Clark Street, Chicago.
Willard, E. W.	Newport, R. I.
Williams, E. B.	Palmer House, Chicago.
Williams, Giles,	New York City.
Wilson, John L.	Windsor Hotel, Chicago.
• Winship, James,	
Wolcott, Alexander,	Chicago.
Wood, Alonzo C.	240 Lexington Street, Chicago.
Wright, George S. ·	
Wright, Truman G.	Racine, Wis.
Yates, H. H.	Chicago.

THE RECEPTION.

AT an early hour, upon the evening of Tuesday, 27th May, 1879, the settlers of Chicago, prior to 1840, began to assemble in large numbers in response to the invitation of THE CALUMET CLUB, at the Club House, corner of Michigan Avenue and Eighteenth Street, and the members of the Club were there to give them a cordial greeting. By 8 o'clock, there was an assemblage of Chicago's pioneers that exceeded in number the expectations of the most sanguine.

Mr. COBB called upon Rev. STEPHEN R. BEGGS, the oldest living Chicago Clergyman, born in 1801, who was here in 1831, to make a prayer.

Mr. BEGGS responded as follows:

Oh Thou who inhabited eternity, we, Thy children, the workmanship of Thy hands, and the purchase of Thy blood, bless Thee for this occasion. We bless Thee for all the privileges that we enjoy and have enjoyed. Under this roof are assembled many who have helped build up this city, and consecrate many churches and perform many good works therein; and we invoke Thy blessing upon them. We thank Thee that the savages have, in so short a time, given way to civilized man, and that where ignorance and barbarism so recently prevailed we now have churches, schools, railroads, and telegraphs. We ask Thy blessing, not only upon the old pioneers here assembled, but upon the whole people of Chicago, and especially upon those in authority. Watch over this city, we pray Thee, and make it a great moral force, setting a good example to all the cities of the world, and aiding to bring millions to Christ. May her progress be still onward, and may she become as noted for temperance, law, and order, and every Christian virtue, as for her commercial enterprise.

We particularly ask Thy blessing, oh God, upon the members of this CALUMET CLUB, who have shown this appreciation of the merits of the fathers of this city, and may they use their organization to continue the good works which their fathers have begun, and labor to promote Chicago's advancement in wealth, learning, temperance, morality, and pure and undefiled religion. And, if we the old settlers may never meet again on earth, may we all meet in Heaven and enjoy Thy presence forever. All of this we ask for Christ's sake. Amen.

At the close of the prayer, Mr. COBB stated that it would be gratifying to the audience if Mr. BEGGS would give his experience in early Chicago.

Mr. BEGGS said:

GENTLEMEN:—My age and infirmities are not my only embarrassment here to-night, for in 1868 I published a book detailing my early Chicago experience, and a repetition of which here would be injustice to others whom I, in common with yourselves, wish to hear to-night. Some of you I know have read that book, and others, undoubtedly, have read some of the many extracts which your newspapers have made therefrom. Under this twofold embarrassment, you must excuse me from making remarks which I otherwise would be happy to make. I should do injustice to my own feelings, however, if I did not express my thanks to THE CALUMET CLUB for their invitation to be present this evening, and my gratitude to Divine Providence for sparing my own life for an occasion like this, where so many of Chicago's pioneers are assembled in fraternity. I commenced preaching in Indiana in 1822. My Conference then embraced the States of Illinois, Indiana, Missouri, and Arkansas. In the fall of 1830, I was sent by the Bishop to supply the churches in the Tazewell circuit in Illinois, which embraced the entire country north of the Sangamon River to Peoria, and east to the head waters of the Big Vermillion River, a circuit of 300 miles around, and I endeavored to preach every day. In the summer of 1831, I planned a visit to Chicago, holding two Camp-Meetings on the way, the first at Cedar Point and the second at Plainfied where I now reside. From the latter place I came in company with Father Jesse Walker

SPEECH OF REV. STEPHEN R. BEGGS.

to Chicago, and was invited to the room of Elijah D. Harmon in Fort Dearborn, whose sons are among the invited guests here to-night. At my first meeting, which was in that room, I had a congregation of twenty-five. My next service was in the log school-house north of what is now Washington Street, on the first block west of the river, upon or near what is now Canal Street, and near Wolf Point. I invited all to come forward who wished to enroll themselves in the Methodist Church. Ten responded. Among them were William See, who was made class-leader, who moved to Racine, Wisconsin, and died there; Elijah Wentworth, Jr., the first coroner of Cook County, who died at Galesburg, Illinois, 18th November, 1875; his mother, Lucy (Walker) Wentworth, who died at Chicago of cholera, 22d July, 1849, and his two sisters, Mrs. Charles Sweet, now of St. Joseph, Michigan, and Mrs. Elijah Estes, of Milwaukee, Wisconsin, whose daughter is now the wife of Rev. Isaac Lineburger, at Dixon, in this State. This same log school-house afterwards served as chapel and parsonage for the itinerant clergyman. Here were his kitchen and his parlor.

At the Methodist Conference, held at Indianapolis, 4th Oct., 1831, I was appointed to Chicago, and held my first Quarterly Meeting in January, 1832, being the first ever held here, and there was also the first Methodist communion service. Mr. T. B. Clark, of Plainfield, carried provisions upon an ox sled to sustain the people through the Quarterly Meeting. Thus did I commence my work in Chicago. Please accept my thanks, gentlemen, and excuse me from speaking further.

Mr. SILAS B. COBB stated that the President, Gen. ANSON STAGER, had been unexpectedly called away, and he would therefore, as Chairman of the "Old Settlers" Committee of THE CALUMET CLUB, introduce to them a gentleman, who was more familiar with addressing public assemblies than himself, to express the object of the Club in giving this reception, and its pleasure at the numerous attendance. This Club was organized 27th of May, 1878. During the one year of its existence, it has given art, scientific, musical, and social receptions; but it remained for it to achieve its greatest success in the line of entertainments by doing honor to the remaining few of the founders of Chicago on this, the first anniversary (May 27, 1879) of its establishment in its Club-House.

I will now introduce to you Gen. HENRY STRONG.

GEN. STRONG then made the following address of welcome:

FELLOW-CITIZENS:—You, the "Old Settlers" of Chicago, we give you hearty welcome here to-night.

It has seemed to us especially fitting that this Club, whose name is the symbol of peace, should give this public expression of honor and gratitude to the men who founded, if not a political empire, still, an imperial city; imperial in in all those higher powers which now control the world, in education, and commerce, and manufacturers, and all the arts of peace; in everything most admirable in the life of a people, founded upon the security which peace affords.

I appreciate the honor of the duty imposed upon me, in the absence of its President, by THE CALUMET CLUB, to stand before you, the survivors of the founders of this great city, and to express the satisfaction and pleasure we feel in extending to you this formal welcome and uniting our congratulations with yours, as we contemplate the splendid result of your enterprise, your courage, and your faith. We only wish that our room permitted us to invite to meet you here thousands of others of your fellow-citizens, who would gladly unite with us in this friendly greeting.

I see before me here to-night the survivors of the men who have principally contributed to make Chicago one of the powers of the earth, not as an independent State, it is true, but none the less a power, and a power all for good, whose benefactions are felt all over the civilized world, as every ship that crosses every ocean, bearing the commerce of the greatest of all nations, carries to the hungry millions of Europe the various food which your commercial enterprise and wisdom have caused to be garnered here; of the men who not only secured the commercial pre-eminence of the city, but who, deeply impressed with the truth that the highest civic greatness cannot be attained by wharves, and warehouses, and marts of trade alone, but must rest upon

, the personal security, the intelligence, and the morality of the citizen, were careful to lay broad and deep the foundations of free and universal education, and gave the earliest encouragement to every association for the promotion of every department of science; of the men, also, who were leaders in developing every public enterprise,—in moulding the jurisprudence of the State—and largely to whose innate love of liberty this great Commonwealth is indebted that the foot of the slave never stained her virgin soil, and that, in her earlier history, resisting the encroachments of the slave power, she continued a free State, and in the end gave to the Union the President who freed all the States, and the General who commanded and conquered armies greater than Marlborough, or Napoleon, or Wellington ever saw.

You left your boyhood homes in the older States to found in a wilderness by this beautiful lake a commercial metropolis, surpassing in all that constitutes the highest municipal achievement any and all of the renowned cities of antiquity, and, even within the lifetime of its founders, rivaling the great Capitals of Europe, which date far back in the early centuries of our Christian era.

We are told in classic story that when the founder of Rome had selected the spot upon which he would build the city, he measured the circle of its proposed circumference by a line made from the hide of a bullock; and thereon erected a wall of stone for the protection of its future citizens. He little thought that the small area so defined and platted would prove but the nucleus of the "Seven-Hilled Rome" of the Cæsars, to whose power all the nations should do homage; whose standards would be borne in triumph wherever there was a people to conquer or treasure to acquire, and whose literature and language have come down to us through all these centuries as pure and authentic and full of life as if written but yesterday, the ever-enduring monument of her imperial greatness.

So methinks when you, the youthful pioneers who founded Chicago, first laid out her village streets in 1830, on the swampy borders of yonder sluggish stream where it joins the lake, and erected here your humble homes, while all around you was primeval nature; or, when later, in 1837, you extended over that less than half section of land a city charter, you little dreamed that you would behold grow up about you, in your day, a city more than rivaling, in the noblest municipal accomplishments, the vaunted greatness of the mistress of the ancient world. You erected no walls of stone to protect your citizens. You sent forth no conquering standards to replenish your coffers with the spoils of nations, but, guarded by the security of law and cultivating the virtues of peace, you have seen the infant city distance in her mighty strides to greatness everything the world has hitherto beheld.

No such municipal achievement was ever known on earth, and all the stories of Oriental and classic fable have been more than realized in this Western wild.

It is said of Athens that when Cecrops decided the right to the possession of the Acropolis in favor of Athenæ and against Neptune, that all the gods concurred, and the city was ever after under the especial protection and fostering care of the Goddess of Wisdom, of Arts, and of Science. Yet Heroditus, the contemporary of Pericles and Thucydides and Sophocles, describes the Athens of the golden age, and in her highest glory, aside from her public buildings, as a squalid city, with mean and dirty dwellings for her people. It is true that splendid temples were erected even upon her harbors, but justice was sold in her courts, the citizen was without personal security or abundant food, education was a sham, and all the warehouses that lined the three harbors of that most celebrated commercially, of all the classic cities, contained not half the grain of one Chicago elevator. Tacitus, writing in the first century of our era, says of London, that it was even then a "great place of trade and merchandise." Yet you, who are still in vigorous manhood, have seen the little prairie town, which its chronicler describes as "presenting no cheering prospects, and containing but a few miserable huts," within your life-time rise to such pre-eminence that in her system of public education, in the general intelligence and personal comfort of her citizens, and as a distributing commercial metropolis of those products of the soil most necessary for the support of mankind, take the lead and now maintain it, of that the most wealthy, the most populous, and the most powerful, of all the cities of the globe, ancient or modern, upon whose growth twenty centuries look down.

But so it has always been that Empires, States, and cities have been founded by heroic men, who have had the ambition to better their fortunes, and the courage to risk and endure perils and privation, and the faith to trust a destiny their own bold enterprise should carve out.

More than forty years ago, Harriet Martineau, who was here, wrote of the then Chicago: "It is a remarkable thing to meet such an assemblage of educated, refined, and wealthy persons as may be found there living in such small inconvenient houses on the edge of the wild prairie."

When you founded this commercial empire upon the border of the great natural highway of lakes and rivers extending from the Valley of the Mississippi to the Atlantic seaboard, and in the midst of a larger area of rich arable land than ever surrounded any other city on the earth, you demonstrated your sagacity by recognizing that profound truth in political economy, that the natural wealth of the adjacent soil is the surest foundation of municipal prosperity. Were London surrounded as Chicago is, by 300,000 square miles of soil rich as the Valley of the Po, the future of England would not be hanging in the balance to-day, as it is. Were the thin and sterile plains of Germany like in quality of soil to the rich alluvial prairies of Illinois, Bismarck would not to-day be exhibiting the remarkable spectacle of the greatest Imperial Chancellor urging upon the Legislature of his country the adoption of a duty upon food, to protect her exhausted soil from the competition of Chicago wheat. Were the sunny hillsides of Normandy, Brittany, and Lorraine covered with the deep black loam of Iowa, Kansas, and Minnesota, Republican France would not to-day be crying out against the invasion of American breadstuffs. A few years ago, when it cost three cents per ton per mile, during the greater part of the year, to carry Chicago wheat, and beef, and pork to the seaboard, and before that era when the cultivator and the reaper took the place of the hoe and the cradle, the self-contained statesmen of Europe hardly knew of our existence, and they put their noble fingers all over the map of the United States, and Canada too, when they would be looking for Chicago. They have found it now. And now, when Chicago wheat, and corn, and beef—both fresh and salted—and pork, and lard, and butter, and cheese, and everything that feeds mankind, are hurried to the seaboard, both by rail and water, at less than one-half of a cent a ton' per mile, and whole fleets enter the harbors of Europe laden with the product of your young Empire, these political financiers of the old monarchies wake up to the knowledge of the fact of the existence of the wonderful young city, which seems to be exhaustless in its resources, and is disturbing the balance of trade throughout the world. And to-day you founders of Chicago witness the strange if not anomalous spectacle of your municipal bantling throwing into commotion the three leading nations of Europe, and causing their hoary statesmen to take down their long-shelved industrial creeds, and even to revise again what were supposed to be the postulates of political economy; and all Europe, wonderful to relate, is discussing the re-enactment of corn-laws.

When we contemplate these astounding results, how our incredulous minds turn back to verify for themselves the almost fabulous story of the date and origin of such a municipal prodigy; to try to discover the succession of events and their cause, which have produced this miracle of civic growth and power. And, sure it is, we find your story true. You were a part of Peoria County but a little while ago, and some of you, gentlemen, before me were here, when Archie Caldwell brought from the Commissioners of that county his license to keep a tavern in Chicago, and to charge six and one-quarter cents for a gill of whiskey, and twelve and one-half cents for a night's lodging. That was a first-class hotel then. You doubtless often sampled that whiskey (to keep off the ague, to be sure), reposed upon those spring-beds, and admired the wolf so artistically painted upon the tavern-sign?

We have also the written evidence of your primitive condition, when officeholders were so scarce that Richard J. Hamilton had to bear the accumulated burden of Recorder, Clerk of the Circuit Court, Notary Public, School Commissioner, and I don't know how many others—a veritable *e pluribus unum* of dignities. And, were it not destroyed by the fire, we could also prove by the record that less than forty years ago your local school tax was only $685; and that conservative Mayor, Chapin, wished to convert the "big school-house," as he called it, into a big insane asylum in which to confine Kinzie, and Scammon, and Foster, and Jones, and the other pioneers in education who insisted upon *large* provision being made for the education of the coming thousands of the youth of Chicago.

Were they living, I would call also Heacock as a witness—the sagacious, enterprising, "Shallow-Cut" Heacock—the fundamental canon of whose hydraulic faith was that water would not run up hill. He was right, and you *boys* had to knock under, or the canal would not have come. And Garrett, too, Auctioneer Garrett, him of the prophetic soul, who, with Abraham's faith, predicted the future greatness of Chicago, founded the Garrett Biblical Institute of Evanston, and, when short of change, was wont to send back to his laundress to be rewashed, the shirts he could not redeem; who indulged in silent oaths at the stupidity of Rees and Kimball, and others of his incredulous friends, who would not permit him to make them rich by conveying to them for $20 per acre land now in the very centre of the city, to be paid for, too, when they should be able to pay for it.

But we have the living witnesses here to-night. Hubbard, Gurdon S. Hubbard, the oldest of this Trojan band; and Beaubien, the Apollo of the early settlers; and Caton, and John Wentworth, and Scammon, and Drummond, and Skinner, and Hoyne, and Blodgett, and Grant, and Morris, and Goodrich, and the Burleys, and Cobb, and Walter, and Arnold, and Raymond, and King, and Williams, and the Wadsworths, and Beecher, and the Kimballs—Mark and Walter, and Laflin, and Dickey, and Van Higgins, and Carpenter, and Carter, and Gray, and Stewart, and the Rumseys, and Stearns, and Boone, and Freer, and Taylor, and Wright, and Eldridge, and Follansbee, and Gale, and Botsford, and more than one hundred others whom I may not stop to name, gathered from all parts of the land,—the men of that little log and clapboard village, from some of whom we shall hear to-night the story of that miracle of municipal progress.

And there were the women, too,— the noble, faithful women, your wives, who nursed the infant Chicago, and who, in all these years of waiting, shared your sacrifices, lightened your burdens, and sustained your faith. I wish they could be here to-night; for I know I speak the sentiment of every heart in this Club when I say we deeply appreciate and shall never forget, the equally important share they had in promoting in every worthy way the prosperity of the youthful city. They would be thrice welcome here.

Gentlemen, you saw the infancy of this city, and you see it to-day. Yesterday a hamlet; to-day a continuous city, covering an area of more than fifty square miles. Yesterday, not a single vessel had entered this port. Now more vessels enter and leave this port every year in the season of navigation than in the same months enter all three of the largest Atlantic ports. Yesterday, you built your houses of logs. Now the lumber that is yearly sold in Chicago would freight a continuous line of vessels 250 miles in length, and would load a freight train 1400 miles long. Yesterday, you could not give away a lot of ground. Now, every week there are more voluntary sales of real estate than in all the cities of New York, Philadelphia, and Boston, and I think I might safely throw in St. Louis and Cincinnati. These are prophetic sales, too; prophetic of future growth, for the purchasers are largely from the other cities I have named.

They talk of bankrupt Chicago. The largest loaning agency in Boston, who has also loaned millions of dollars here, said, not long since, that he only wished Boston loans paid their interest as promptly as Chicago's.

Yesterday, you fattened your yearly pig and made your own pork. You bought and sold none. Now, the hogs and the hog-product sold and made here yearly exceed thirteen hundred million pounds, a line of living hogs that would reach nearly a quarter around the globe. The lard made by one Chicagoan is known the world over. Yesterday, the neighboring farmer dragged in through the mud his few bags of wheat or corn. Now, one hundred and thirty million bushels of grain are sold yearly in Chicago,—I mean are actually received from the adjacent country. Instead of the back room of the store where you kept your wheat, there are now elevators with a capacity of fifteen million bushels.

Yesterday, the aggregate sales of stock, and merchandise, and manufacturers' products of all kinds, were less than ten thousand dollars yearly. To-day, they are seven hundred and fifty million dollars. The annual sales of one dry goods house are over twenty million dollars. Yesterday, the prairie-schooner was your only means of transportation. Now, twelve thousand vessels yearly enter your port, and ten thousand miles of railway have their head-quarters here, not including the Eastern lines, nor lines in the far West not controlled here, but which look to this city as their market. Yesterday, was heard the anvil of the single blacksmith. Now, may be heard the hammers of the largest rolling mill corporation in the world, employing in all its branches over four thousand men, and supporting over twenty thousand people, with its capital stock above par, while even Pittsburg mills barely survived the late panic. Yesterday, you waded through mud between your stores and houses. To-day, there are 122½ miles of contiuous street railway; 650 miles of streets; 7.8 miles of boulevards; and 844 acres in improved parks. Yesterday, you dug your shallow wells in the surrounding swamp. To-day, you have 430 miles of water mains, and are annually supplied with 19,564,000,000 gallons of the purest water in the world. Yesterday, you groaned under a debt of seven thousand dollars, and feared municipal bankruptcy. To-day, the obligations of the city, if non-taxable, would stand on a par with the bonds of the Federal Government, and the municipal debt is less per capita than any other large city on the continent.

I hurriedly mention these few facts, showing what clothes your infant wears, because some of you now residing at a distance are not aware how the child has kept on growing since you left. Why, they thought they had destroyed it by fire a few years since. I'll tell you now (otherwise you might not know it by what you see) they did burn it up; that is, they burnt several hundred million dollars of buildings and property. But the men you left here, and others that came in, built it right up, better than before; for you can't burn pluck, and enterprise, and courage, and faith. They are the indestructible gifts of God, *and the best legacy you, the founders of Chicago, shall ever leave your children.*

I wish time would permit me to speak of other evidences of growth, in education, in charities, in art, of intellectual and moral growth. I only give you this assurance that your child stands well up toward the head of the form, and that one of the largest publishers in America told me that of a certain class of books, of a desirable kind, Chicago is the best market in the Union.

But I cannot let this occasion pass without a word of tribute to the honored dead, your friends and fellow-pioneers in the great work of civilization, which you and they accomplished. Kinzie, and Ogden, and Clarke, and Garrett, and Brown, and Sherman, and Hamilton, and Heacock, and Dole, and Hallam, and Turner, and Newberry, and Peck, and Dyer, and Brainard,-and Egan, and Lisle Smith, of the silver tongue, and Wilson, and Calhoun, and Manierre, and Butterfield, and Couch, and Harmon, Elijah Wentworth, Sr. and Jr., and Clybourn, and Moore, the Millers, and Spring, and Russell, and Murphy, and Loyd, and Curtiss, and Woodworth, and Hogan, and Hubbard, and Dyer, and a long roll of noble, manly men, have gone, and them we lament to-night. But the recollection of their virtues we will ever cherish, as we do of the founders of the Republic. Their work lives after them, and will live for all time. When the stately buildings which now adorn our marts of business and our beautiful avenues shall have crumbled to dust, the memory of these heroes of peace shall survive, forever fresh in the hearts of the citizens of Chicago. If, indeed, it be permitted to mortals in the dim hereafter to visit again the scenes of their labors here below, then are they with us here to-night; and you, spirit-band of Chicago's founders, you also, we welcome at this reunion.

Hail, ye noble shades! The forms that once ye wore among us have been laid by the side of yonder lake, whose waves shall sound your requiem through all the coming years, but your spirit shall ever dwell here to inspire us and all who shall come after us, the beneficiaries of your labors, with your enterprise, your patience, and your faith. And you who still survive: I utter the heartfelt prayer of every member of this Club in wishing that you may long be spared to witness the prosperity of our beloved city.

At the close of Gen. STRONG'S address, Mr. SILAS B. COBB stated that he was confident that every person present was desirous of hearing from ex-Chief-Justice CATON, and he should therefore call upon him not only to respond to Gen. STRONG, but also to act as President during the remainder of the evening.

SPEECH OF HON. JOHN DEAN CATON.

Ex-Chief-Justice JOHN DEAN CATON took the Chair and said:

GENTLEMEN OF THE CALUMET CLUB: The pleasing duty has been assigned me by my associates of years gone by of expressing our feelings toward you for your kind words and generous hospitality. It is a task I feel quite unable to perform. Words are wanting which will adequately express the sensibilities which are awakened in the bosom of each one of us, whom your generous forethought has brought together here; who, forty years or more ago made the little hamlet of Chicago their home, and devoted their energies to laying the foundations of this great city. It is gratifying to us to know that as we are passing down the road that ends where we cannot see, those who are rising up to take our places in the labors of life feel kindly toward us, and appreciate what we have done, or at least attempted to do. As I look about me and see gathered here friends of so many years ago, I am transported back to the time when we were all young. Even then there were old men here, at least so they seemed to us, among whom I may recall Col. Jean Baptiste Beaubien, Dr. Elijah D. Harmon, and John Wright. They have long since passed away, but their names should never be forgotten. The old men called us boys then, with more main-spring than regulator, but we thought we were well-balanced men. You call us old men now, but we feel somewhat boyish still. It is a pleasant retrospect to go back in memory forty years—let me go back forty-six years, when I here set my stake and commenced the business of life. There were then not two hundred people here. I was an old resident of six weeks' standing before two hundred and fifty inhabitants could be counted to authorize a village incorporation under the general laws of the State. Col. Beaubien presided at that meeting, and at his request I sat beside him as prompter, for official honors and responsibilities were new to him.

When we had attained the dignity of a village-corporation, with the wild waters of the lake on the one hand, and the broad and brilliant prairie, still untouched by the husbandman's plowshare, on the other, we thought we were a great people, and even then though feebly discounted the future of Chicago. Of those who were present at that memorable birth, I rejoice to see many here present. How can I express our feelings of gratitude to that Divine hand which has so long sustained us, and bounteously lengthened out our days and again brought us together under conditions of so much happiness, and in the enjoyment of so goodly a measure of health. I think I can count twenty at least who were here forty-six years ago, when Chicago had no streets except on paper; when the wild grass grew and the wild flowers bloomed where the court-house square was located; when the pine woods bordered the lake north of the river, and the east sides of both branches of the river were clothed with dense shrubbery forests to within a few hundred feet of their junction. Then the wolves stole from these coverts by night, and prowled through the hamlet, hunting for garbage around the backdoors of our cabins. Late in 1833, a bear was reported in the skirt of timber along the South Branch, when George White's loud voice and bell—he was as black as night in a cavern, and his voice had the volume of a fog-horn, and he was recognized as the town-crier—summoned all to the chase. All the curs and hounds, of high and low degree, were mustered, with abundance of fire-arms of the best quality in the hands of those who knew well how to use them. Soon bruin was treed and despatched very near to where the Rock Island depot now stands. Then was the time when we chased the wolf over the prairies now within the city-limits, and I know some here were of the party who pursued one right through the little hamlet and onto the floating ice near old Fort Dearborn. O, those were glorious times, when warm blood flowed rapidly, no matter how low stood the mercury. Then in winter the Chicago River was our skating-rink and our race-course. Let me ask John Bates over there if he remembers when we skated together up to Hard Scrabble—where Bridgeport now is—and he explained to me by pantomime alone, how the Indians caught muskrats under the ice? And let me ask Silas B. Cobb if he remembers the trick Mark Beaubien played on Robert A. Kinzie to win the race on the ice that winter. See now how Mark's eye flashes fire and he trembles in every fibre at the bare remembrance of that wild excitement. This was the way he did it. He and Kinzie had each a very fast pony, one a pacer and the other a trotter. Mark had trained his not to break when he uttered the most unearthly screams and yells which he could pour forth, and that is saying much in that direction, for he could beat any Pottawatomie I ever heard, *except* Gurdon S. Hubbard and John S. C. Hogan. The day was bright and cold. The glittering ice was smooth as glass. The atmosphere pure and bracing. The start was about a mile up the South Branch. Down came the trotter and the pacer like a whirlwind, neck and neck, till they approached Wolf Point, or the junction, when Kinzie's pony began to draw ahead of the little pacer, and bets were two to one on the trotting nag as he settled a little nearer to the ice and stretched his head and neck further out, as if determined to win if but by a throat-latch. It was at this supreme moment that Mark's tactics won the day. He sprang to his feet in his plank-built pung, his tall form towering above all surroundings, threw high in the air his wolf-skin cap, frantically swung around his head his buffalo robe and screamed forth such unearthly yells as no human voice ever excelled, broken up into a thousand accents by a rapid clapping of the mouth with the hand. To this the pony was well trained, and it but served to bring out the last inch of speed that was in him, while the trotter was frightened out of his wits; no doubt thinking a whole tribe of Indians were after him, and he broke into a furious run, which carried him far beyond the goal before he could be brought down. Hard words were uttered then, which it would not do to repeat in a well-conducted Sunday School; but the winner laughed and fobed the stakes with a heartiness and zest which Mark alone could manifest.

There is an inspiration in the memory of those glorious days of fun and frolic which quickens the pulse to full youthful vigor, and now to see so many of those around me who were the life and soul of those hilarious times, transports me back to them, and makes me feel as if no long years of toil had rolled along since then. We forget for the moment the intervening time, and remember only the broad unbroken prairie, which then extended for miles around the spot where this hall stands. But you must not think that all our time was spent in fun and frolic.' Our sports were but episodes, while our days and nights were spent in labors inspired and sustained by vigorous health, indomitable will, and a full appreciation of the life-long task before us. We felt and knew that wisdom and energy and industry could alone build up such a city as its geographical position seemed to require. The spirit manifested by those who commenced the work would be likely to make its impress upon the teeming throngs which were already hastening to join us from the East and the South, and the wonderful work wrought by those who joined and came after us, and which have just been so truthfully and so eloquently described, we flatter ourselves were in part at least the followings of what we began.

To us of the olden time, who as your guests feel ourselves so much honored, contrasts are continually presenting themselves. *Then* and *now* ever present themselves side by side. Here I commenced my judicial career at the age of twenty-two as a justice of the peace. On the 14th of July, 1834, a judicial election was held in this town, including the village and surrounding country, for one justice of the peace. The canvass was very warm and active by the friends of the two candidates, though no party-politics were involved in the contest, as I think there never should be in judicial elections. One candidate received 172 votes, and the other received 47 votes. But 219 voters could be found in Chicago and vicinity. Probably this was the last election ever held here when every voter came to the polls. Indeed, I regret to say that the most-enterprising and thorough-going men here have rarely taken time to go and vote, and their example has been too largely followed, though not by the baser sort. At the last presidential election, three years ago, Chicago polled 62,448 votes, and yet a large number of voters took no interest in the matter, or at least took more interest in their stores or their shops. I doubt if much more than two-thirds of the voters in this City have voted since 1840. How can we resist noticing the contrast between 219 in 1834, and 62,448 in 1876, especially when we remember that the latter number was heavily handicapped.

On that same 14th of July, an event occurred of a commercial character which should render it memorable, and deserves to be recorded. On that day the first commercial vessel that ever passed the piers into the Chicago harbor—the "Areadne," Capt. Pickering. Early on that morning the friends of the successful candidate assembled at the piers, which consisted of a few wooden cribs, and dragged the schooner across the bar into deep water, where all got on board and sailed in her up the river to the Point where the election was held, shouting merrily, and were answered by those on shore manifesting an appreciation of the important event. She was gaily decorated with all the bunting which could be raised, and we thought presented a splendid appearance, the rigging manned by all who could climb the shrouds. This kindled an enthusiasm which lasted till the last vote was polled, and no doubt contributed more to the success than the merits of the candidate. The most active and efficient man on that day, as I remember, was the late George W. Dole, who was always thoroughly in earnest, whether electioneering for a friend or attending to his commercial affairs. His memory should be ever cherished, and his name never forgotten when the founders of this City are recalled.

The contrast in the hotels and of the mode of living in Chicago, is scarcely less striking. The first night I slept in Chicago was in a log-tavern, the name they went by then, west of the junction of the rivers, kept by W. W. Wattles. The next day, I learned that the best entertainment was to be had at the crack boarding-house of the place, kept by Dexter Graves, at five dollars per week. It was a log-house near the middle of the square just north of the present Tremont House. If it was a log-house I assure you we had good fare and a right merry time too. There were seven beds in the attic in which fourteen of us slept that summer, and I fear we sometimes disturbed the family with our carryings on o' nights. I know of but one of those fourteen boarders besides myself now living. Edward H. Haddock knows who slept with me in that attic. Haddock was a sly fellow then, for before one of us suspected what he was at he made sure of the flower of that family, and a real gem of priceless value she was, who still survives to promote the happiness of those around her. Young ladies were in demand here in those days.

The first frame-tavern ever built in Chicago was by Mark Beaubien, upon whose geniality advancing years seems to have no influence. I am sure there are some here present who were then his guests. There he kept tavern, to use his own expression at the time, like—the Judge hesitated.

(A voice—"How?") "Shall I say it, Mark?" (Mr. Beaubien answered, "Yes!") Well, then, he said he kept tavern "like hell!"

To go back to that primitive time, and to think of those who are gone and those who are left, we may gratefully acknowledge that a very large proportion have been spared through so many years of active life. Gen. Strong has recalled the names of a number of the prominent early settlers of Chicago who have passed beyond the reach of your hospitality. Allow me to recall the names of two who have been taken from the ranks of my own profession, and who came to Chicago the same year with myself—1833. Their learning and their talents would have made them conspicuous at any bar. All who knew them will join me in paying a tribute of respect to the memories of Giles Spring and James H. Collins. Besides these there were several other lawyers who located in Chicago during the same year, among whom I may mention the name of Edward Casey, a most genial gentleman. All of these are long since gone, and I alone am left to represent that earliest Chicago bar.

[Here a question was raised by some of the old-timers as to whether Mr. James H. Collins came in the year 1833, but Judge Caton settled it, stating that he finished his legal studies in Mr. Collins' office in New York, and came directly thence to Chicago, when he wrote back to his former preceptor an account of the country, on the receipt of which Mr. Collins made his arrangements to come West, and arrived in Chicago in September, 1833, and in February following he entered into partnership with Mr. Collins in the practice of the law, constituting the firm of COLLINS & CATON.]

Resuming, Judge CATON said: To those who have not been eye-witnesses, it seems incredible that in the adult lifetime of so many of us here present a city of half a million of inhabitants has grown up from nothing, and that what was then a rich wild waste for five hundred miles or more around, has been subdued, cultivated, and populated by millions of hardy, industrious, and intelligent agriculturists. The marvel is the *growth* of the *country* rather than the city. The latter was compelled by the former, and indeed has never kept pace with it.

Still, to those who have witnessed all this, it seems more like a dream than a reality. To those who have not witnessed the growths of cities and country in this occidental land, many can hardly believe that he who addresses you now opened the first office for the practice of the law in Chicago. They have often called me the father of the Chicago bar, and proud I am of such a progeny. In numbers they are truly great, and in ability, in learning, in integrity, and in patriotism I will proudly compare them with any other bar in the United States. I have ever tried to so bear myself that no one should blush at the mention of my name, and I most gratefully acknowledge that they have always shown me a filial affection, ever treating me with the greatest respect and confidence, omitting no opportunity to do me honor. This is a consoling reflection, and a sweet experience in the decline of life.

Would time permit, it would not be unbecoming in me to follow my friend who in your behalf has extended to us so cordial a welcome in the great changes which have been here wrought in so short a time—for remember that the period of one human life is but a day in the life of a people; but I must forbear. Really it seems like mystery that what was but yesterday a very little village—for it seems but yesterday that I was a very young man—has to-day grown to be so great a city. Sometimes despotic power has builded cities in the frozen North and in the genial South; but a Peter and a Constantine, with national resources, could never equal the magic results which we have here witnessed as the voluntary works of freeborn enterprise, here in the temperate zone, where no ancient civilization had left its work. It lacks but antiquated ruins and crumbling columns to persuade the traveller that he is in some great city of the old world, where modern architecture has wiped out many of the evidences of departed grandeur and supplied its place with the improvements of later times. But the end is not yet. If we saw the very beginning you too have seen but the beginning. When the youngest man among you shall have passed through the active scenes which lie before him, and shall feel that his work is nearly done, he will stand amid a succeeding generation, and tell those who shall have arisen to take the places of him and his contemporaries, of what he remembers of the present time as of the beginning of Chicago, or at least of its early youth. Then our voices will be hushed, to be no more heard forever, and may we not fondly hope that he will still kindly remember us, and that we here lived and labored before his time. So, too, may we hope that this CALUMET CLUB may flourish those forty years or more to come, and that its members still will stretch forth the hand of welcome to those who shall survive from now to then, as cordially as you have extended your courtesies to us.

If we have talked only of Chicago and its progress, we must not forget that Chicago is not phenomenal, but it is the whole great West that is phenomenal. We have other great cities in this grand, magnificent valley, whose growth, whose enterprise, and whose greatness, should equally command our admiration; many of whose early founders are yet spared, to hear the expressions of gratitude, and to receive the honors which they so richly deserve. Let us not say that there is a rivalry between these great cities of the West; but there is a noble emulation as to which shall do most for the honor and the glory of our beloved country.

Nothing would be so agreeable to me as to talk to you by the hour of ancient Chicago, when the wild waters of the lake, on the one hand, were rarely vexed by the ships of commerce, and the wild flowers which covered the broad prairies, on the other, were undisturbed by cultivation, and uncropped by flocks and herds — save the wild deer that roamed at large over their broad bosoms; but I fear you will think I am becoming a little senile in my enthusiasm. Especially do I like to talk of the olden times, when I see around me so many of those old-time friends, with many of whom I have not clasped hands for twenty or thirty years. Here is my old friend, Mark Beaubien, of whom I have so often spoken—because he is so worthy of mention, and because his name is so closely interwoven with all our sports and joyous gatherings, when we were all young together. He used to play the fiddle at our dances, and he played it in such a way as to set every heel and toe in the room in active motion. He would lift the sluggard from his seat, and set him whirling over the floor like mad! If his playing was less artistic than that of Ole Bull, it was a thousand times more inspiring to those who are not educated up to a full appreciation of what would now create a *furör* in Chicago; but I will venture the assertion that Mark's old fiddle would bring ten young men and women to their feet, and send them through the mazes of the dance, while they would sit quietly through Ole Bull's best performances—pleased, no doubt, but not enthused so that they could not retain their seats. That was long years since; but if he has that same old fiddle still, he can, I doubt not, draw the bow now in such a way as to thrill those at least in whom it will awaken pleasing memories of days and nights when young blood coursed wildly and joy was unrestrained. To show you that this is so, and how he did it then, I call on him to play some of those sweet old tunes, if he has that same old fiddle yet.

After the close of his remarks, the President said:

The old settlers, and the members of THE CALUMET CLUB, are very desirous of hearing from Judge HENRY W. BLODGETT, who is the oldest settler among us, so far as residence is concerned. He came here in 1831, and we would like to know something of Chicago at that early day.

Judge BLODGETT came forward and said:

MR. PRESIDENT: If there were not so many old settlers here to catch me at it, I might venture to draw another kind of long bow from that our friend, Mark Beaubien, has been exercising, and tell you some stories about the time before Judge Caton came here and opened his law office. As it is, I am warned by these witnesses, and must keep within the limits of fact. But I doubt whether I ought to consume much time here this evening on the score of being an old settler, for I am not certain that a lad, who, even as long ago as 1831, was taken from the valley of the Connecticut and brought by his parents to the western shores of Lake Michigan, can by such involuntary action claim to be an old settler, when compared with those who came even later, of their own free will, upon the impulse of their own courage and enterprise. If it were needed, I can bear witness to the wonderful growth of this city, already so graphically and truthfully portrayed. As I have said, I do not claim to be an old settler, and do not admit being an old man; but in this crowd I rather claim to be one of the boys. And yet my memory reaches back to the time when every man, woman, and child in Illinois north of Ottawa, and east of the Rock River, were gathered here in little old Fort Dearborn, and we only mustered enough men and boys over ten years old to carry a hundred muskets. To-day, the territory from which those settlers had fled for refuge to the Fort now numbers nearly a million inhabitants, who will compare for intelligence, public spirit, and average wealth with the population of the same area in any country. I mention this fact only for the purpose of emphasizing the statements in regard to the growth of this city and its adjacent territory, which have been so appropriately put together by Gen. Strong. That within the brief years compassed by my recollection, this whole empire of the Northwest, with this city as its commercial centre, should have sprung into existence, is a fact worth pondering upon; and those who pioneered the way to such results have certainly some good grounds for boastfulness. But is it not about time that we stopped talking about infant Chicago, about this wonderful prodigy of youthfulness? Have we not passed the stages of childhood and adolescence, and is not Chicago now a mature and developed city, no longer a problem, but a fixed fact? A place that has suffered the vicissitudes this community has passed through—that has stood no less than three financial panics and reverses, one "Chicago fire," and innumerable small ones, has certainly had experience enough to be matured by this time. So let us cease talking about young Chicago, as if we were still trying an experiment, and its ultimate result was a matter of doubt, and count our future as assured and guaranteed.

As short speeches only should be in order on an occasion like this, I will only add that I am rejoiced to meet so many of the old settlers here to-night, and am thankful that the members of THE CALUMET CLUB have by their generous and hospitable thoughtfulness brought this reunion about, and I trust we may have more such meetings in the future.

At the close of Judge BLODGETT's remarks, the President said:

I will next call upon Judge JAMES GRANT, now of Iowa, who came here and joined me in the practice of the legal profession in 1833.

SPEECH OF HON. JAMES GRANT.

Judge GRANT responded:

MR. PRESIDENT: To-night I have not voice enough to talk; I have not ears enough to hear. Every face that I see is a reminiscence of the past. Every eye that I behold brings back to me pleasant memories of what has gone before. Forty-five years is a long period in the life of a man in any age, or any country; but in Chicago it is a short lapse of time. You cannot count its progress by years or by days. Like Minerva from the brain of Jove, it sprang into maturity from its existence. A Chicago man never dies. You may die, I may die, and those who come after us may die, but the Chicago man, like the king, and like liberty, is immortal.

Fifty years ago it required forty days on horseback (the then most expedient way of travel), to go from Raleigh, the capital of North Carolina, to the few log-cabins on Lake Michigan, where I made my early home. The same journey I have done by the railway and steam engine in forty-eight hours; and the same means of commerce has, in thirty years, converted the log huts into an imperial city, built of marble, with five hundred thousand enterprising people, more potent in the world's history than Rome in the days of Augustus Cæsar. So, in all parts of civilized society, the railway, by the annihilation of space, has increased the use and duration of the time which is allotted to our existence to such a degree that we live longer and accomplish more in fifty years than in the nine hundred years of the age of Methuselah.

THE PRESIDENT then called upon Hon. JOHN WENTWORTH.

Mr. WENTWORTH responded:

MR. PRESIDENT: I was gratified to receive an invitation to attend this union of the old settlers of Chicago, and still more gratified to find enclosed in the invitation a printed list of the others who had been invited. It is with pleasure also that I learn that since the list was printed, others, whose residence at that time were unknown, have been invited. I have long wanted such a list, a list of our living pioneers, a directory of our living historians. Men often call upon me to make enquiries concerning past events;

and, when I feel unable to give them correct answers, I try to think of some person now living who can. But it has been difficult to tell who were living; and, if living, where they lived. Now I have a directory of the living. This list furnishes me with an index to the voluminous unwritten history of Chicago. There is scarcely an event in our early history with which some person, whose name is here recorded, is not associated. Every name I look at suggests some chapter in our history. I prefer to speak from this list, as the room is too crowded for me to recognize all, and yet there are many who are prevented by the various necessities of life from attendance. I feel safe in saying that all absent old settlers are with us in spirit, and will look with interest for our proceedings. I have tried to shake hands with all, and I have noticed no one yet whom I have not readily recognized. And all have seemed to know me, and I think there is no one here who has not at some time voted for me for some position, dependant upon his concurrence with my views upon the measures of public policy then pending.

When I first entered the room, I exclaimed "History, Chicago's History!" and whilst I was remarking to some older settlers than myself, that I had lived in the State long enough to have shaken hands with all our Governors but three, I noticed in the crowd Col. Gurdon S. Hubbard (who was here in 1818) who must have shaken hands with the other three. And now my eye catches a glimpse of Col. Edmund D. Taylor who has shaken hands with every Governor Illinois ever had, State or Territorial. I tell you, Mr. President, if I am to make a short speech, it is going to be dangerous to look around, and quite as dangerous to keep looking at this list. Chapter after chapter of our history is flitting across my mind so rapidly that my tongue cannot keep pace with my thoughts. Col. Taylor must be the oldest Illinoian in the room, if not in this part of the State. He came here when Illinois was a territory in 1814, containing a population of about 12,000 people, and there were a few slaves then; and the capital was at Kaskaskia. He was elected to the House of Representatives from Sangamon County, 2d August, 1830, when the capital was at Vandalia, and again, 6 August, 1832. He was elected to the Senate 4 August, 1834, and, often participating in our

early canal-legislation; he received a commission from Gen.
Andrew Jackson, as receiver of public monies at Chicago.
In him you see the man who sold at the sale commencing
15th June, 1835, the first acre of land for the U. S. Government in this region, and the very lot upon which we are
now so agreeably enjoying ourselves was sold by him at
$1.25 per acre, and his first sale amounted to nearly a half
million of dollars. Our more recent settlers, who are
accustomed to high-priced lands, will not think this was
much of a sale. But, when they consider the price, they
will appreciate the magnitude of the sale, it being near
400,000 acres. So here to-night we have the first chapter
in our land history. We can here begin at the section-corner. Col. Taylor was born in old Virginia, and he has
not changed his landed jurisdiction much; for he is to-night
in what was once a part of the State of his birth. And
this reminds me that, not long since, some one wrote me
in behalf of the Historical Society of Virginia, asking me
the names of our prominent citizens who had emigrated
from that State. My knowledge of birthplaces has not kept
pace with our directory. So, in ignorance of the present,
I referred him to the past, claiming that, if Chicago was colonized from any quarter, it must have been from old Virginia. I referred him to David McKee whose name is
upon this list. If not here to-night two of his brothers-in-law are, Williard and Willis Scott. He was one of the very
first men who were married in this City. He was married
by the original settler, John Kinzie, 23d January, 1827.
He was the first blacksmith in our City and carried our only
mail once a month to and from Fort Wayne, Indiana.
There was another Virginian, to whom I referred him,
Archibald Caldwell, who kept the original Wolf-Point
Hotel, now living near Kershena, Wisconsin, whom I am
sorry not to see here, but here is Willis Scott (not a Virginian) whose first wife was his sister. Benjamin Hall is a
Virginian whose second wife is a sister of our honored
President, to-night, Judge John Dean Caton. He is now
living at Wheaton, Ill., with a head full of early history.
And our chaplain here to-night, Rev. Stephen R. Beggs, was
born in Rockingham County, Virginia, 30th March, 1801,
the same month in which Thomas Jefferson was inaugurated
President. There may be other Virginians living, but of

the deceased my memory recalls James Kinzie (our first sheriff); his brother William Kinzie; Archibald Clybourne (Justice of the peace in 1831); his father Jonas Clybourne and his brother Henly Clybourne; our early presiding-elder, Rev. Jesse Walker; John K. Clarke, (the celebrated hunter); David Hall; and Samuel, John, and Jacob Miller.

There is another man here to-night who revives in my mind not only a great deal of our City's and our State's history, but of that of the entire North-west. He was at Detroit when Gen. Hull surrendered the American army in 1812. All of you have read the particulars of that surrender; but few of you ever heard of them from an eye-witness. And this may be the last occasion when any of you will be able to look upon a man who was present upon that occasion. So I speak to you of Mr. Mark Beaubien as a gentleman of unusual interest. It is over forty years since I heard his narrative, and also heard him sing a song, in ridicule of the surrender, made by the inhabitants, which he sung in my office yesterday with the same vivacity with which he sung it before our City was incorporated. And he accompanied it with his fiddle—the same old fiddle. And who is there here to-night who has not heard that fiddle? How well it has been preserved we will show you after the refreshments have been finished. We are too old to dance upon an empty stomach. Among my pleasant recollections are those of frolics to the music of that fiddle, made up of Indians, half-breeds, Canadian French, and Americans. And our Indians were no common Indians. They were chiefs with their families. The chiefs disliked to leave us. Long and long after their tribes departed, the chiefs remained; and, when they did go, many would revisit us. Who does not remember Chamblee (Shabonee) and Robinson (Chechepinque), who died amongst us, and Billy Caldwell (Sauganash) who died 28th September, 1841, at Council Bluffs, Iowa, with his tribe—although passing much of his time with us? I remember meeting at Mr. Beaubien's, Sauganash and Shabonee. Mr. Beaubien told the story of the surrender of Detroit by Gen. Hull, and its recapture by Gen. Harrison. Then Sauganash and Shabonee gave an account of the battle of the Thames and the death of Tecumseh! When the Americans made the attack, Tecumseh, Sauganash, and Shabonee were sitting upon a log in consultation. Shabonee was aid to Tecumseh, and Sauganash held a commission as captain in the British army under the name of Billy Caldwell. A wonderful man was this Billy Caldwell, and there are several in this room who have been upon hunting excursions with him. He owed allegiance to three governments without any renunciation. He was Captain Caldwell of the British army, Esquire Caldwell of the State of Illinois, and Sauganash, Chief of the Pottawatomies. He was appointed justice of the peace 18th April, 1826, being the first appointment after Chicago was set off from Fulton County to Peoria.

Many of us remember the part played by Mr. Beaubien and his fiddle at the marriage of the daughter of the Indian chief, Joseph Lafromboise, to Thomas Watkins, a clerk in the post-office, where I, for the first time, saw the original "war-dance." The company was made up, in about equal numbers, of Indians, half-breeds, Canadian French, and Americans. A few days thereafter, we remember that an elegant party, for those times, was given in honor of the newly-married couple by a nephew of Mark Beaubien, and the fiddle came to the front again. His name was Medore B. Beaubien, and he was a member of the first board of trustees, elected in 1833, nearly a half-century ago. He is the earliest-elected officer of Chicago now living, and the bride of that occasion, now living, is his second wife. He is the business agent of the Pottawatomie Indians, and is the mayor of the city of Silver Lake, Kansas. His name is upon this list, as also is that of his partner, in Chicago mercantile business in early times, Valentine A. Boyer.

Our friend, Mark Beaubien, erected the first hotel upon the south-side, and named it after his friend Sauganash; and it was there that I took my dinner, upon the first day of my arrival here, 25th October, 1836. Near his hotel, he established the first ferry across the Chicago River. At his house, the first election for trustees was held on 10th August, 1833. Some one may ask if I wish it understood that the whole population was running after Mark Beaubien and his fiddle, in those days. The facts would be otherwise, if I did. For here were Philo Carpenter, Grant Goodrich, both now present, (to say nothing of the many noble dead) who were organizing bible societies, temperance societies, home and foreign missionary societies, and

otherwise sowing the seed which has made our City the most reverential and moral city of its size in the world—
—the City of churches—the City where ambitious and destitute congregations send for their best preachers, and from which vacant dioceses select their best bishops. I was much interested in a recent lecture upon early Methodism in Chicago, delivered by Grant Goodrich. It is often said that the good die young. The gray hairs and bald heads in this assemblage contradict the assertion. The old settlers of Chicago are passing their threescore years and ten, and are still invoking Providence to point out to them paths of usefulness.

I see Willis Scott here, who had to go to Peoria in 1830 for his marriage license. There are several persons here who were here when the first steamboat arrived to bring Gen. Scott and his troops for the Black-Hawk war. Here is Judge R. N. Murray, who was one of Gen. Scott's soldiers, and marched under him to the Rock-River Valley. There are persons here who have lived in Fulton County, Peoria County, and Cook County, and never changed their residence. If John Watkins* is not here, he ought to be, for he taught our first district-school, and was the first clerk of our first school-district, and is living near Joliet. Philo Carpenter and Grant Goodrich were upon the executive committee of our first bible-society, formed in 1835, and it would be difficult to name any good cause in which they and Tuthill King were not engaged. Deacon Carpenter was the master-spirit in forming the first anti-slavery society, and knew better than any other man the safest, if not the shortest, route from Chicago to Canada. There are several attorneys here who were in active practice before our City was organized, and both the members of the firm of Goodrich and Fullerton yet live here. And here is J. Young Scammon, who published the second volume of the Illinois supreme-court reports, and now we are upon our ninetieth volume. If our State had adopted the plan of most states and only published one volume each year, he would be much over one hundred years of age by this time. And here is ex-Chief-Justice John Dean Caton, whose opinions have helped make up those reports. And here are the names of Joseph N. Balestier, Isaac N. Arnold, Andrew

* See letter of John Watkins in Appendix.

SPEECH OF HON. JOHN WENTWORTH. 51

J. Brown, Henry W. Clarke, Hugh T. Dickey, Grant Goodrich, James Grant, Thomas Hoyne, Alonzo Huntington, Buckner S. Morris, Mahlon D. Ogden, Mark Skinner, and Wm. B. Snowhook. Here are physicians who were here before our City was organized: Dr. D. S. Smith, Dr. L. D. Boone, (since mayor), and Dr. John W. Eldridge, who was, in 1840, elected one of the presidential electors who cast the vote of this State for Martin Van Buren. He was one of the first men to appreciate me. For he went to a Democratic congressional convention in the winter of 1837–8 and voted for me when I was constitutionally ineligible, being but twenty-two years of age. Stephen A. Douglas secured the nomination, and the man who introduced me to him, Isaac Cook, who kept, at his Eagle, the most fashionable resort for Illinois politicians, is with us to-night. And here are a dozen men who heard the first public discussion ever held in this City, that between Stephen A. Douglas and his successful competitor, John T. Stuart, of Springfield, the only man now living, of either branch of congress, who entered congress from Illinois before I did. Dr. Eldridge, however, got his man in 1843, and Douglas also had to wait until I went with him. Our first medical college was chartered in 1837, and here to-night are three of the original trustees, Grant Goodrich, Edmund D. Taylor, and John D. Caton. How many old merchants are there here to-night on this list? Philo Carpenter, Tuthill King, Devotion C. Eddy, Mathew S. Molony, Horatio G. Loomis, Wm. H. Adams, Wm. Osborn, Gurdon S. Hubbard, J. Milo Strail, Eli B. Williams, Oren Sherman, E. S. Wadsworth, W. H. Taylor, Edwin Blackman, V. A. Boyer, James E. Bishop, Samuel J. Surdam, Edmund D. Taylor, Stephen F. Gale, M. L. Satterlee, Ed. K. Rodgers, Sidney Sawyer, M. B. Beaubien, Walter Kimball, Jabez K. Botsford, Joel C. Walter, George Chacksfield, Benj. W. Raymond, T. B. Carter, and others. Col. Hubbard, in 1835, advertised that a schooner had just arrived bringing him fresh goods only twenty days from New York. And here is Arthur G. Burley, the oldest continuous merchant in our City. I found him a clerk in the store of John Holbrook when I came here. He was in business in 1838, and I still buy my crockery of him. He was burned out in 1839, as well as in 1871, going into the fire like the salamander and coming out like the phœnix.

This list furnishes the index to the whole history of our fire-department. Late in 1835, Col. Gurdon S. Hubbard engaged our first hand-engine in New York, but not in time for it to reach Chicago that year. Capt. John M. Turner was the first foreman of Hook and Ladder Company No. 1, and was promoted from that place to be our first chief-engineer, 11th March, 1837, the oldest now living, and here are the names of some of his successors: Alanson S. Sherman, Luther Nichols, and Stephen F. Gale. We have here to-night eight members of the original fire-company organized in 1835, viz.: Jabez K. Botsford, Isaac Cook, Silas B. Cobb, Charles Cleaver, John L. Wilson, Wm. H. Taylor, Grant Goodrich, and Tuthill King. Would you not like to see them running with the machine now? The fire company held its meetings in the Presbyterian church, for whose dimensions, as compared with our present engine house, I refer you to Deacon Benjamin W. Raymond. Our early clergymen are well represented on this list also. Besides our venerable chaplain, who tells us he was here in 1831, I see the name of Rev. Jeremiah Porter, who was here in 1834, and of Luke Hitchcock, and Flavel Bascom, who came after. There were no baptismal fonts in those days. But purer than old Jordan ever was, the Chicago River was good enough for immersion. I remember upon one cold day early in February, 1839, seeing seventeen immersed, and Chicago's honored architect present here to-night, John M. Van Osdel, was one of them.

This list shows that our early surveyors are nearly all living. Here is the name of Amos Bailey, who was county-surveyor before our City was organized, and of Asa F. Bradley, his successor, who held the office until 1849, and James H. Rees, our first city-surveyor, and here by my side sits Alex. Wolcott, our present and long-time surveyor, elected in 1855, a settler of 1834, who has waded every marsh in our county; and, whilst sitting in his office, can describe the precise spot where we can find any section-corner. And here also is the name of E. B. Talcott, who was town-surveyor under the government of the Trustees. Here is the name of Augustine D. Taylor, who saw the first printing-press landed at our Chicago harbor in 1833; and here is Walter Kimball, who was in the office when the first newspaper, the *Chicago Democrat*, was struck off, Oct. 28, 1833.

Too late for him to attend, an invitation was sent to Capt. Morgan L. Shapley, at Meridian, Texas, who was employed at Buffalo in June, 1833, to come here and assist at the commencement of the works at our harbor. A. V. Knickerbocker should be here, son of the first clerk of the harbor-works, who continued in that capacity many years. And here is C. B. Dodson, one of the first contractors. Lt. A. A. Humphreys, now general and chief of engineers at Washington City, who took charge of the harbor-works as early as 1838, could give us some very pleasant reminiscences of early Chicago, and so could Col. Jesse H. Leavenworth, who succeeded him. I do not find the name of Jefferson Davis upon this list, nor see him present. But he was engaged in the survey of Lake Michigan about 1832, and I was surprised to learn, upon my first acquaintance with him, how many of our early settlers he knew and how kindly he spoke of them. He contended that Calumet instead of Chicago should have been the city.

You have the whole history of our canal here. Besides Col. Edmund D. Taylor and Col. Gurdon S. Hubbard who participated in the early canal-legislation, you should remember that one of the first board of canal trustees is present in the person of Col. Hubbard himself, who was elected representative from Vermillion County in this State, 6th August, 1832. And here is E. B. Talcott, one of the first engineers. There was a grand celebration here upon the 4th of July, 1836, and the people all went to Bridgeport to see Col. W. B. Archer (for whom Archer Avenue is named), as acting commissioner take out the first shovelful of earth, and two of the marshals, Walter Kimball and Edmund D. Taylor, are now present. And there are a great many of the original canal-contractors here present, and others are upon this list. Now we are in the habit of considering contractors a sort of business-tramps, making their homes wherever they overtake a job. But not so with our contractors. Representing in Congress the entire canal line from Chicago to La Salle, I think I had a personal acquaintance with all of them. With a little reflection, I think I could point out the job of each man. And how few ever left our State! They mostly remained among us and have ranked among our leading citizens; one governor, several mayors, senators, representatives, taking an active part in developing our resources and in advancing our moral and educational interests. They were a very far-seeing body of men also. Do you not suppose that George Armour had his great elevator in view when he was digging the canal? Here is Gen. Hart L. Stewart who knew if he took a boy for the canal's first congressman, he would finally grow to it! He was vice-president of the congressional convention which assembled at Joliet, May 18th, 1843, over thirty-five years ago, our deceased Lt.-Gov. John Moore being president. And while upon the subject, let me remark that here is W. T. Burgess, one of the secretaries, and also upon this list Hugh T. Dickey, the other, and also Col. W. B. Snowhook, Henry W. Clarke, Col. Julius M. Warren, and Judge R. N. Murray, who were delegates. If my twelve years in Congress were of any service, you can thank these men who helped set the ball in motion.

I see the president of one of the old boards of town-trustees, Eli B. Williams, and one of his colleagues, Asahel Pierce, here, and in justice to that board it should be said that it was wound up without owing a dollar. And that is the way that every corporation should wind up. But we have had scarcely another wound up in the same way. I do not see Nelson R. Norton present, who built our first draw-bridge upon Dearborn Street in 1834; and the old steamer Michigan, Capt. Chelsey Blake, was the first to pass through it. He also built, in 1835, the sloop Clarissa, the first sail-vessel launched on Lake Michigan. He resides at Alden, Minnesota. He was the whig candidate for alderman from the old sixth ward at our first charter-election, and is the only man upon that ticket now living.

If you ask what were the principal entertainments in those days, I would answer: The meetings of the debating society, in which all the citizens took an interest. Col. Hans Crocker, now living at Milwaukee, Wis., was the first secretary in 1835. In that year, one of the questions was: "Are the frequent Indian disturbances owing to the clemency extended to the Indians by the General Government?" Grant Goodrich, now present, lead the debate in the negative, and I think he would do so again if the debate should be opened. As this question has never been settled, and as the man who led the debate in the affirmative is not living, I will appoint Major-Gen. Philip H. Sheridan to take his place. We had occasional theatrical performances. My earliest recollection in this respect runs back to the time when Joseph Jefferson, who has gained such a reputation as Rip Van Winkle, made his appearance at about ten years of age. Little did we then think that the lad that we were applauding as a matter of encouragement, was to receive upon his merits the applause of the nation. When I hear of Joe Jefferson's fame, I cannot forget that it was Chicago people who gave him his first "send off." There are many persons here present who remember when the Indian tribes all through the North-west assembled at Chicago to receive their annuities. And still more remember when the Indians where finally removed from all this region of country, and our Fort Dearborn was abandoned by the national troops.

There are many persons here to-night, who attended the first meeting called to take into consideration the provisions of our city charter, on the evening of 23d January, 1837. All went pleasant until we came to the limitation upon our city debt. Hon. Henry Brown, the historian, the name of whose son, Andrew Jackson Brown, is upon the list, in the advocacy of a liberal policy, contended that the child was then living who would see fifty thousand people here. A gentleman, whose name I afterward learned was Walter L. Newberry, was very active in opposing the debt-policy; and, when the negative vote was called for, he seized me by the coat-collar, as I was sitting, and said, "Stand up, young man," I responded, that I was not a voter. He asked, "Don't you intend to live here, and don't you expect to get rich?" I admitted that I did. He gave my collar an extra pull, and said, "Well then, stand up! Give these men the power, and they will abuse it, until they bankrupt us!" And up I stood, and I have been thus standing on similar votes and occasions ever since. Ever after, upon all matters of taxation, Mr. Newberry and I acted together. I became associated with him in banking, in rail-roading, in the board of education, and in many other capacities, and found him an inveterate foe to the generally-received doctrine, that a man's moral responsibility was any less for his public and corporate action than for his individual action. He believed in saving as well as in earning, and was one of the very few, if not the only one of our reputed millionaires, who proved to be such after his death.

His farewell words to me were of the same meaning as his first: "Keep up the fight!"

Our first mayor, Wm. B. Ogden, is dead; but upon this list is the name of our first city-clerk, Isaac N. Arnold; and you all see the city-clerk under our fourth mayor, Thomas Hoyne. And the publisher of the first corporation newspaper is now addressing you. Here are two of the members of our first board of aldermen, John Dean Caton, of the third, and Asahel Pierce, of the fourth ward, these two wards then embracing the whole west-side. In Judge Caton's ward, there were but 38 votes; and in Mr. Pierce's 59, making only 97 votes on the entire west-side. There were only 709 votes in the entire City. The house where the first election in the fourth ward was held, then known as the Green-Tree Hotel, afterward the Chicago Hotel, just west of the Lake-Street bridge, n.-e. corner of North-Canal Street, is the oldest building in our City. It was, at one time, the best place for public meetings and parties on that side of the river.

The name of the second mayor, Buckner S. Morris, is upon the list. But Edward H. Hadduck and Eli B. Williams, of the first ward, and Grant Goodrich of the sixth, who were upon his board of aldermen are present. Mr. Hadduck was one of the judges of election of the first ward at our first municipal election, the year before; and is the only one of the judges at that time now living. I was challenged because I was a boy, and Mr. Edward H. Hadduck administered the oath. Strange as it may seem, the same charge of being under age met me again when I first run for congress, and I suppose I was the youngest man in congress when first elected. I did not begin to fill up, although as tall as I am now, until about 35 years of age, and my whiskers were so late in coming, and so many persons were going into the business that I never cultivated the crop.

Our third, who was also our sixth mayor, Benjamin W. Raymond, is here to-night with both his aldermen from the third ward, in 1839, Ira Miltimore* and William H. Stow; and also Charles McDonnell, of the second, and Alanson S. Sherman, of the third ward, in 1842; and this is the same Sherman who was mayor in 1844. Here are the names of Julius Wadsworth, of the first ward, and John Gage, of the

* Died 10 June, 1879.

SPEECH OF HON. JOHN WENTWORTH. 57

third ward, in 1840, and here is the name of John Davlin, of
the first ward, and I see present Chas Follansbee, of the first,
and Peter Page, of the second, of the board of 1841. Here
is the name of Hugh T. Dickey, alderman of the first, in
1843. Here is Elihu Granger, one of the aldermen from
the fifth ward, in 1844. Here are J. Young Scammon, of
the first, in 1845, Levi D. Boone, of the first, and Wm. M.
Larrabee, of the sixth, in 1846; Robert H. Foss, of the
fourth, William B. Snowhook and James Lane, of the ninth,
in 1847. John C. Haines, of the fifth, in 1848, afterward
mayor, William H. Adams, of the third, and Amos G.
Throop, of the fourth, in 1849, and Isaac L. Milliken, of the
second, in 1850. I will carry the details no farther. I
wanted to show you in the destruction of so many records,
how much of personal memory there is to substitute for
them. Although the mayors prior to and including 1850
are all dead but three, we have here some member of every
board covering that period, and there are a large number,
about thirty here, who have been aldermen since. And
Alderman Throop, of the board of 1849, is in the council
now. And here is Amos Grannis, an old settler, his col-
league, of the present year, from the fourth ward. It seems
that young America yet has some appreciation of the old
settlers. I will add, however, that we have seven other
mayors here on this list of old settlers, Walter S. Gurnee,
Charles M. Gray, Isaac L. Milliken, Levi D. Boone, John
C. Haines, Julien S. Rumsey, and myself. I notice in this
room, five of our sheriffs, Isaac Cook, William L. Church,
John L. Wilson, Timothy M. Bradley, and John Gray. Also
we have three postmasters, Hart L. Stewart, Isaac Cook,
and Samuel Hoard; four state-senators, Edmund D. Taylor,
Samuel Hoard, Henry W. Blodgett, and John C. Haines;
one speaker of the house of representatives, Elijah M.
Haines, and six members of the house, Isaac N. Arnold,
Thomas Drummond, Augustus H. Burley, J. Young Scammon, Mark Skinner, and Hart L. Stewart. Three judges of
probate are here, Walter Kimball, Mahlon D. Ogden, and
Thomas Hoyne. Two members of congress are here, Isaac
N. Arnold, four years under Abraham Lincoln, and myself
twelve years, at different periods, commencing with John
Tyler and ending with Andrew Johnson. Were it appro-
priate I could give some very early history, having served

with men who were born before the American Revolution, and with one, John Quincy Adams, who heard the guns at the battle of Lexington. *Sufficit* to say, that I have represented twenty-two counties running east to the Indiana State line, west to the Mississippi River, north to the Wisconsin State line, and south to the Quincy, Springfield, and Wabash districts. It takes twelve men to represent that territory now.

Here I see William Lock, S. J. Surdam, and James A. Marshall, members of the first masonic lodge ever organized in Chicago, and the eighteenth in the State, old "LaFayette," with Carding Jackson, master; and here are members of the first odd fellows lodge also, and the ninth in the State, old "Union," A. G. Burley, S. B. Walker, E. W. Densmore, Jerome Beecher, D. Horton, and H. H. Husted.

Here are two members of the first board of water-commissioners, H. G. Loomis and A. S. Sherman; and one member of the first board of sewerage-commissioners, Sylvester Lind.

Two U. S. district-attorneys, Thomas Hoyne and Mark Skinner are here. Two State's-attorneys are here, James Grant and Alonzo Huntington. In 1840, July 10th, John Stone was hung. Mr. Huntington prosecuted, at the trial, and here is Robinson Tripp, who, with myself, was upon the jury. But, prior to that, in 1835, there was another murderer, Joseph F. Norris, who took a change of venue to the nearest county, then Iroquois, where he was convicted and hung, 10th June, 1836, from the limb of a tree. James Grant, now present, was the prosecutor, and the late Henry Moore, with whom I commenced the study of law in this City, defended him. I need not tell you that we have one supreme-court judge here, John Dean Caton. And then we have here, or upon this list, three circuit-court judges, or judges under different names with equivalent jurisdiction, Hugh T. Dickey, Buckner S. Morris, and Mark Skinner. One U. S. district-judge, Henry W. Blodgett is here. And who does not know that that veteran in jurisprudence, our U. S. circuit-judge, Thomas Drummond is here, his original commission bearing the signature of "Old Rough and Ready," General Zachary Taylor. And this suggests, what a museum of commissions we could establish here to night, and full of all sorts of historical reminiscences. Col. E. D.

Taylor would bring forward his commission from General Andrew Jackson, as receiver of public monies. And Ed. H. Hadduck his commission for the same office from Gen. W. H. Harrison. Jackson, Harrison, Taylor! What suggestive names! And then our U. S. District Judge, Henry W. Blodgett, present to-night, could bring forward his commission from the more recent General Ulysses S. Grant. And Mark Skinner could bring his as U. S. district-attorney; and Eli B. Williams, as register of the Chicago land-office from John Tyler; and Hart L. Stewart, as postmaster, from James K. Polk; and Wm. B. Snowhook, as collector, of the port, from Franklin Pierce; and Isaac Cook, as postmaster, from James Buchanan; and Samuel Hoard, as postmaster, from Abraham Lincoln. The appointees of President Van Buren, and Acting-President Millard Filmore are numbered with the dead. Acting-President Andrew Johnson knew not the old settlers, and President Rutherford B. Hayes has not recognized us as yet. If he wants his name in such a museum there is still an opportunity.

I should have stated that the first collector of our port is here, Col. William B. Snowhook. And here is the history of the first railroad built from Chicago, from its organization to its final "gobbling up." I see my colleagues, Benj. W. Raymond, Silas B. Cobb, and Edward K. Rodgers, here. And here are the names of William M. Larrabee, our secretary, and Edward B. Talcott, our superintendant. The modern railroad-men change our name from old settlers to old fogies, as we paid our debts and never omitted a dividend. We paid our president $1000, and I audited the accounts for the love of it.

The first bank was started here in 1835, the Chicago Branch of the Illinois State Bank, and here I see three of its original directors, Gurdon S. Hubbard, Edmund D. Taylor, and Walter Kimball. And here is also Ezra L. Sherman, the teller.

Our school boards are well represented here, although I see no one here whose appointment bears date prior to mine, in 1838. Isaac N. Arnold is still in the board, and here are also Edwin Blackman, Charles N. Holden, Philo Carpenter, Samuel Hoard, and Mark Skinner, once of the board.

Who does not remember the old auction-house of Garrett, Brown & Co., where the mellifluous voice of the late mayor, Augustus Garrett, was heard every evening in selling lots all over the north-west. Here is the name of Nathaniel J. Brown, of that firm, if any one wants to know the extent of the town-lot business in those days.

If any of you wish information of wars, I would say that here are men whose experience leads them to the war of 1812, Black-Hawk war, and several other Indian wars, and the Mexican war, as well as to the war of the rebellion. The Mexican war is considered a small affair as compared with the latter; but its importance will be highly appreciated when we consider that it gave us our Pacific possessions, and that the Pacific railroad was its legitimate consequence.

I notice among those who have given us this splendid entertainment several young men, and it is but natural that they should enquire if we had no society-men in those days. Our early settlers were generally society-men, but they never let society interfere with their business. If our accomplishments have not already been demonstrated, perhaps we can make a more pleasing demonstration, when to the tunes of Mr. Beaubien's fiddle, that same old fiddle, we shall ask you to join in the dance of your parents and grandparents. Oh! that that fiddle could speak! How many pleasant memories would it revive. I notice a gentleman here who was a model of a society-man. He was at his place of business promptly every day and at parties every night. After sunset, he would go farther to attend a party, dance longer, and be back at his place of business earlier the next morning than any other man in the City. He has lived in pleasure and to profit. He brought nothing here; his notes never went to protest, and now he has nearly means enough to pay the debts of almost all our modern society-men. If the society-men of these days would but follow his example, work as well as play, save as well as earn (to use a granger-phrase), they would find a great deal more corn on their Cobb. I notice also here the ever-pleasant countenance of our old-time master of ceremonies, the Lord Chesterfield of the frontier. When DuPage County was created from Cook, our people did not object to losing the territory, but they solemnly protested against setting off Col. Julius M. Warren. But, when the new county elected him to the legislature, Chicago found it had an additional member. Every hotel-keeper within a radius of fifty miles would give, at least, one party during the year, and as no party could be a success without Col. Warren, he always had the naming of the days, and when his name was printed upon the invitations as manager, no weather could prevent a crowd. Nor must I forget James A. Marshall, who is in our midst, the great innovator upon old-fashioned dances. He introduced the quadrille, and those who were too old to learn, objected to coming to a frolic and then having to sit still while the quadrille was danced. The matter was compromised at first by having quadrilles while supper was being eaten, thus making Mr. Marshall and his followers eat at the second table. Mr. Beaubien soon found out that he could call quadrille changes while fiddling, and whoever went into his hotel by day could hear him practising, calling out, "Balance all," "Forward two," "Cross over," "Chassé," "Dos-à-dos," etc., until the Indians, half-breeds, servant-girls, stage-drivers, barkeepers, and all his guests, were well posted. Then our friend Marshall stirred up a furious tempest by introducing the waltz. Most parents disapproved of it, their daughters rather liked it, but the clergymen opened a tremendous battery upon it. Previously they had not objected to the attendance of the members of their church. Sometimes, they would even permit their daughters to attend our parties and would come themselves to accompany them home. And they would come early. For they liked our suppers.

Gentlemen, in my zeal I have forgotten the length of time I have been talking. Nothing is so near my heart as the restoration and perpetuation of our history destroyed by the fire. I want to re-establish the old landmarks, and here is the material to do it with. There never will be so many old settlers together again. I look upon this list as an index to our history. I see different and interesting chapters in every countenance. Let each one write out what he remembers and leave it with his friends or, what is better, with the Historical Society; being as particular as possible as to dates.

You called upon me for a speech; but I have preferred to inaugurate a class in early history. Here, in this list of invited guests, is my roll of scholars. I have prepared blank text-books, and named a few chapter-headings, under which you can write your experience or add other chapter-headings, and write under them as your experience may best dictate or your memory best serve you. And, if you but do what you are able to do, in this aspect, posterity will be under obligations to THE CALUMET CLUB of Chicago, for bringing us together to-night, as profound and many times more lasting than even·we are under for its unparalleled hospitality.

THE PRESIDENT called upon Judge GRANT GOODRICH.

Judge GRANT GOODRICH responded:

Mr. PRESIDENT: The first thing which struck me on entering this room to-night, was the contrast which those present presented, to the persons composing the first gathering I ever attended in Chicago; here nearly all I see are gray-headed men, then, there was not one to be seen.

It was a happy thought of this Club to project this meeting, and it has been most felicitously carried into execution. It is fitting that those who laid the foundations of such a city so recently, who were active in shaping and promoting its marvellous career, should meet to exchange fraternal greetings, and congratulations over the changes which have been wrought here within a period so recent. If those men, who by dessolating wars, have destroyed kingdoms, states, and cities, deserve to be remembered, surely those who founded such a city as this, and settled and developed the surrounding country, covering it with fruitful fields and happy homes, may well rejoice over their achievements, and deserve to be remembered for the good work which they have done.

How changed, Mr. Chairman, is all here, and around here, since you and I first looked upon it. In May, 1834, beside the garrison, and the former employés of the American Fur Company, there were scarcely one hundred inhabitants. So far as I can remember, there were but eight frame dwelling-houses in all the territory now covered by the City. The timber extended down from the south branch of the river, to near Madison Street, and the undergrowth, to near Randolph and the Public Square. On the north-side, it came to near the main river, as far as Clark

Street, then, shaded off toward the lake to Indiana Street. No street, south of Lake, was distinguishable, and in the spring, it was doubtful whether every street had a bottom. Between here and Naperville, where a few families had located, there were but two dwelling-houses. In a southerly direction, but one at Blue Island, until you reached Yankee Settlement, on Hickory Creek, where a few eastern immigrants had made their claims, and built their cabins. The broad prairies, those garden fields of nature, lay with all their wealth of verdure and fertility, bright with many-colored flowers, heaving in ridges of billowy green, waiting for the immigrant's herds and plow. No wonder, when opened to the pioneer, they were settled so rapidly. Our friend here, Col. Julius M. Warren, will remember that in early June, 1834, that beautiful prairie which lay between the Dupage and Fox Rivers, had not a single house upon it, but before the summer was gone, it was covered by settlers, as a flock of pigeons would light down upon a harvest-field.

It is not wonderful that those who see Chicago to-day, with all her commercial, mercantile, and industrial facilities, cannot realize its condition, as it was 45 years ago. These men around us to-night are the survivors of those young men, whose enterprise and perserving industry, whose bold conceptions and fearless execution of sagacious plans, largely contributed to make Chicago what she is, the marvel of the world.

As you have said, Mr. Chairman, those young men who came here with us, and have gone to their graves, deserve and should receive a share of whatever meed of praise is due to the pioneers of Chicago. A more enterprising, energetic, intelligent, and determined band of young men never embarked their fortunes upon the sea of life. They were full of hope and pluck; prepared to endure cheerfully, the privations and labors necessary to win success. Mutual dependence begat among them a beautiful spirit of fraternity and brotherhood. They had faith in each other and faith in Chicago. Its future greatness became their theme of thought and conversation, and the inspiration of great plans and deeds.

I did not, like Judge Blodgett, come here involuntarily, but of set purpose. It came about in this wise: When studying my profession, I belonged to a debating society, and the question was proposed, "where the waters of the great lakes could most advantageously be connected with those of the Mississippi"? In looking over the maps, I hit upon Chicago, and reading all I could find upon the subject, resolved that when I should graduate I would seek my fortune there.

We had toils, struggles, deprivations, and disappointments; but they were borne with cheerful courage, and have been crowned with grand and successful results. We sometimes had our fun too. Our highest expectations hung upon the construction of the Illinois and Michigan Canal. In the winter of 1834-5, Gurdon S. Hubbard, John H. Kinzie, and others, visited the legislature at Vandalia, to urge the passage of a bill to commence the work. They succeeded in getting it through the house of representatives, and securing the pledges of votes enough to carry it in the senate; but, two senators·who had agreed to support it, changed their minds, and secured its defeat. The indignation at Chicago was hot and fierce, and she must give some signal expression of it. A cannon was procured, effigies of the offending senators made, and placed on the bank of a cellar, where the Tremont House now stands, and John and Robert Kinzie, and others, performéd around them the ceremonies which the Indians practised around prisoners, devoted to mockery, torture, and an ignominious death, after which one was shot into fragments from the mouth of the cannon. The other one was laid upon a rude bier, and carried upon the ice on the river, escorted by Geo. White, as master of ceremonies, the town bell-ringer and the only negro here. The effigy was then placed over a can of powder, which was exploded, up-heaving the ice, and blowing the senator high in the air, and tearing him into fragments, amidst the shouts and jeers of the multitude. We were compelled to furnish our own amusements, and this is a specimen of the way in which it was done.

We have passed through great vicissitudes; have seen, and many have felt, the extremes of material prosperity and adversity. To secure the business, growth, and health of the City, we have seen great obstacles met and overcome. I may properly allude to a few of them. The original surface of most of the land on which the city stands, was only

SPEECH OF HON. GRANT GOODRICH. 65

from four to six feet above the river, which was on a level with Lake Michigan.

When an effective system of sewerage became a necessity, the daring plan was conceived and successfully carried out, of lifting the City up six feet, in order to secure it. And such confidence was felt in the skill of the engineers and mechanics having it in charge, that while dwellings, entire blocks of stores, huge warehouses, and hotels, were being raised up bodily, traffic and business continued to be transacted in them without material interruption. So, also, when a supply of pure water became indispensible, a tunnel was driven out two miles under the lake, and an unfailing supply of purest water·was brought and distributed throughout the City. When the passage on the bridges over the river became thronged, and interrupted by the growing commerce upon it, highways were tunneled under the river bottom, and free passage secured. When her commercial and lumber fleets were multiplied beyond the capacity of her rivers to accommodate them, miles on miles of new channels were dredged into the land for their use. When 2200 acres of the City was swept by a tempest of fire, of nearly every store, of every warehouse, and their contents, and of thousands of dwellings, leaving 150,000 of its inhabitants without a roof to cover them, or a bed on which to lie, Chicago's pluck and energy did not fail, but proved equal to the emergency. Her crowning achievement, the rebuilding of the City, is justly entitled to be regarded as the grandest and most marvellous exhibition of human industry and energy the world ever witnessed.

I am glad I have lived to see such a city rise from what it was, to what it is. We ought all to be thankful, that God has permitted us to be actors in such wonderful achievements, and to see the realization of more than our wildest dreams.

I will only add, that I pray that those who may come after you, may leave behind them as creditable and beneficient a record as has been made by the early pioneers of Chicago.

THE PRESIDENT then called upon J. YOUNG SCAMMON.

Mr. SCAMMON responded:

Mr. PRESIDENT:—I wish to hear from so many of the

gentlemen present, whose faces I have not seen before for many years, but whom I saw nearly forty-four years ago, when I came to Chicago, that I shall refrain from making a speech. I shall not make any remarks, except to correct, on my own account, and on account of the old settlers here, an error in the address of which we have listened to with so much pleasure. I wish to tender my thanks to Gen. Strong, for the very eloquent, able, classical, and truly historical address which he has made at this meeting, and to express the wish that it will not be allowed to pass into oblivion, but will be printed in a permanent form, and placed, if not in the archives of this Club, at least, in the archives of the City, and of the Historical Society, and in the libraries of all the old settlers, and of the new settlers who wish to learn and remember the history of Chicago. I wish, in this connection, to correct one or two statements. It was said, that Mayor Chapin recommended the sale of the first great school-building, or of its being converted into an insane asylum, for the purpose of confining gentlemen in it who had been instrumental in wasting the people's money in building "big school-houses." It was not Mayor Chapin who made that proposition. John P. Chapin was one of the most noble men who lived in Chicago. He was an early mayor, but subsequent to Mayor Garrett, succeeding him in office, in 1846, and was one of our largest and most influential and enterprising merchants,—a man who always stood at the front, in favor of every true enterprise, and every measure that tended to improve and extend the power, influence, and prosperity of the City of Chicago.

There is one other man, now departed to his long-home, however, who deserves a great deal of credit, in relation to the schools of the City, and I beg permission to say a few words in his commendation. That man was Dr. Josiah C. Goodhue, and if I recollect right, he was one of the first aldermen of the City. He was one of the committee who designed the seal of the City, which I recollect was called "Dr. Goodhue's little baby." He it was to whom we are indebted very much for our present school-system. The public schools had been tried in Chicago, and proved to be a failure. While he was a member of the first council, —I think every member of the council was democratic,—

one evening he came into my office, which was very near then where it is now, on the south side of Lake near Clark Street, and lamented over the condition of things in Chicago. It was after the panic of 1837, which was vastly worse than the panic of 1873, and everything was very depressed. "Nothing," he said, "could be done here in the West. The people of Chicago had voted down the free school-system." (You will recollect in 1835, the people voted down the first local free-school bill we had obtained from the legislature for Chicago), and he said we could not have any schools. I said, playfully, to Dr. Goodhue, we can have free schools, and if you will put the matter into my hands, I will establish a free-school system that will be satisfactory to the City of Chicago. He said he would do it. I said, "You can not do it; you and every member of the council are democrats, and I am a whig." He said: "That makes no difference. If you will take hold of it, you shall have unlimited power to do what you choose, and the council will sustain you." I said, if he would do that, I would give as much time as was necessary to it; but I said, he could not get the council to agree to it. He said, "I think you are mistaken; I think you can have your own way about everything. I will consult the council, and let you know next week." About a week afterward, he came to my office, and told me that the council were all agreed, and if I would take hold of the matter, I might write my own ordinances and laws, and they would give me supreme power, within all reasonable bounds. I did so. I wish to say this, not for the purpose of recounting anything I have done, but to give to the common council of Chicago, which differed from me in politics, and which you, Mr. Chairman (Judge CATON), was a member, and to Dr. Goodhue, the credit of the first act which culminated in the permanent establishment of the public schools of Chicago. The council put the whole matter into the hands of one of their political opponents, who was then supposed to be an ambitious man, and one who never lost that reputation, until his wings were scorched by the Great Fire, in order to further the great cause of public instruction; and we are indebted now for our excellent school-system to the stone that was first laid by Dr. Goodhue. I wish to say as to the first board, of which I was a member for several years,—

it was selected upon non-partizan and non-sectarian ideas, and served faithfully and conscientiously. The memory of some of its leading members is perpetuated in the naming of our schools.

The first public-school building which was erected in Chicago, was called Dearborn School, and it was on the north side of Madison Street, east of Dearborn. It was built in 1844, while I was in the board.

It was, at that time, the practice to select those who were supposed to be good men for the places of aldermen, and to insist on such men taking their turn in serving the public.

Mr. Edward H. Haddock, one of our oldest and wealthiest citizens, who is here this evening, and who had served a term as alderman of the first ward, came to my house one morning in the spring of 1845, and said: "You must run for alderman in this ward this year; and if you will run, John Calhoun (who was a democrat, and my neighbor,) will run with you, and you shall be elected without any opposition." I said I had too much to attend to, but he insisted and I finally consented to do so. When the thing was made known to the leading men of the whig party, to which I belonged, they said the first ward was the only whig ward, and we ought not to forego our right to put two whigs in the council. I then said I would not run. But Mr. George W. Meeker, who was one of the board of school-directors, while walking with me up Dearborn Street met Alvin Calhoun, a prominent partizan whig, and said to him, we are going to nominate Scammon for alderman to-night. Mr. Calhoun replied, "We can't elect Scammon." Said Meeker, "Why not." He responded: "I have nothing to say against Scammon. He is a good man, except that he goes in for building too big school-houses. The people don't want their money wasted in that way;" and I could not get the nomination, or if I did I could not be elected. The whig nominating convention was held that night at the old Mansion House, on the north side of Lake Street, between State and Dearborn, and I was nominated with very slight opposition. But I declined to run so long as any one was opposed to my nomination. Mr. Haddock then said I had no right to decline; and he offered a resolution, which was almost unanimously adopted, that I should not be permitted to decline. In consideration of the ground of opposition stated to Mr. G. W. Meeker, in my presence as before stated, I concluded to run, and to test the question whether "big school-houses" were unpopular, and to see whether it was true, as Alvin Calhoun had said, "that no one who built great school-houses could be elected." Mr. Calhoun had stated, in the conversation alluded to, that Scammon "was crazy on the subject of schools, and the people would not allow their money to be wasted." I made up my mind I would try that single question, and I got both a larger vote and a larger majority than any man had ever had for alderman in the City; and this seemed to settle the question as to the popularity of big school-houses.

In 1845, Augustus Garrett, the democratic candidate, was elected mayor at the same time; and when Mr. Mahlon D. Ogden, who is now present, and who was also elected an alderman at the same election that I was elected an alderman, and I took our seats in the council, the mayor read his message in which he denounced the extravagant school-policy, and proposed that the public school-house on Madison Street, which was too large to be ever filled with scholars, should be sold or converted into an insane asylum.

I wish to do justice to the memory of the late John P. Chapin and to the memory of Dr. Goodhue, in relation to the great question of public instruction. I am sorry I have not time to allude to other matters, or more than to mention the name of a great man to whom, in my opinion, we are indebted more than to any other, and to whom the whole North-west is indebted for public improvements,— more than to any other man, since I have lived in Chicago —a man who came to Chicago in 1835, William B. Ogden.

If one minute more will be allowed to me, I wish to pay a tribute of respect to one of five or six lawyers I found here in 1835, when I landed upon the then harborless shore of Chicago,—one of our best citizens, who is now lying on a sick-bed on the other side of the river. He and I had an office together over forty-two years ago, precisely where my office is now. He was a man, Mr. Chairman (Judge JOHN DEAN CATON), you knew well. He was the second mayor of Chicago, and elected over a leading democrat, while he was a whig, in a city where the democratic majority was so large that the year before every officer was a democrat, but he had been a partner of Edward Casey before. He was with Judge Goodrich afterward, and you and I know he was the best lawyer ever in the City of Chicago or any other place, on the wrong side of a question that had no merits in it. He not only had that character, but what was better, that of a good lawyer, a good man, and a good citizen, and he made a good judge of our courts, to which office he was elected by the people. I refer to the Hon. Buckner S. Morris. Peace to his last days, and to his memory. I am sorry he is not here. He was one of us in the olden time. We liked him then, and we do not forget him now.

The President then called on ex-Lieut.-Gov. William Bross, who said:

Mr. President:—I lack some nine years of being technically an old settler, that honor belonging only to those who were here previous to 1840. It would not be modest in me, therefore, to make much of a speech, and I will only occupy your attention for three or four minutes to say that although I came here in 1848, after the canal was finished, I have seen every steam railroad built in Chicago; I have seen every horse-railway built, and drove the first spike to fasten the first rail laid on the corner of State and Randolph Streets; I have seen Chicago become a great city, burn up, and built up again. And during these early years of my residence in Chicago, I looked over its early records before the great fire. In 1852–60, I was thought to be the great wild man of Chicago, and everybody said I was publishing all sorts of nonsense about this great City, but I leave it to you, Mr. Chairman, if I ever half kept up with the truth. In the early records is found two or three things of curious interest; one was in reference to friend Beaubien, who kept tavern vigorously, and run the ferry at Wolf Point. His love for his fiddle was well known, and besides he often took part in pony races with his Indian neighbors, and hence, lest he should forget his duty as ferryman, they passed an ordinance that he should ferry the people of Cook County day and night without stopping. Another thing I will mention. We hear a good deal about rapid transit in these days. A gentleman who has been connected with rapid transit from the organization of the City is here to-night, and is connected with it still. I refer to

Mr. Cobb, the President of the Chicago City Railway, who commenced his career early in the history of this City, by putting in a ferry at the enormous expense of $9.60 across the river at Dearborn Street. You see that it has resulted in making him President of the City Railway Company, and one of the solid men of the City.

At the close of this speech, the guests were invited into the supper-room. After refreshments they returned to the original reception rooms, which had been cleared for dancing. Mr. BEAUBIEN took a position at the head of the rooms with fiddle in hand, and the guests all went forward and shook his hand as a valued friend of olden-time, and congratulated him upon his well-preserved appearance and good spirits.

He sung a song, accompanied by his fiddle, in ridicule of Gen. HULL'S surrender, which he learned at Detroit in 1812.

He and Col. GURDON S. HUBBARD indulged in a conversation in the original Indian tongue, which terminated in their giving a specimen of Indian dancing, to the great merriment of the company.

Hon. JOHN WENTWORTH assumed the roll of floor-manager and, with a voice loud enough for the deafest to hear, called upon Col. JULIUS M. WARREN to lead SILAS B. COBB to the head of the hall for "Monnie Musk." He called upon all over seventy-five years of age to form on next, then all over seventy, all over sixty-five, all over sixty, all over fifty-five, all over fifty. He then requested the younger members of the Club to stand back and see how their fathers and grandfathers danced when MARK BEAUBIEN handled the bow.

The "Virginia Reel," and several olden-time favorite dances were afterward gone through with. Many olden incidents were revived, and stories told. And the settlers of Chicago, prior to 1840, took their leave with many expressions of gratitude, and hoping, without reasonably expecting, that some day they might all meet again.

The names of the invited guests are published. Some made no response. The infirmities of age, in some instances, would not permit a response, and there may have been a mistake, in other instances, as to the present post-office address. But of the settlers of Chicago prior to 1840, one hundred and forty-nine registered their names out of the large number invited. And there were several persons who recognized the whole number, and shook hands with them as familiar acquaintances. Many left without knowing that there was a registry being kept. A few called afterward and signed the registry, and all Chicago settlers, prior to 1840, are now requested to do so.

The following tables may be of interest, as showing the places of birth, the years of arrival, and ages of those who signed the registry during the evening:—

PLACES OF BIRTH.

Connecticut	16	Maine	3	New Jersey	3
England	10	Massachusetts	10	N. Carolina	1
Ireland	6	Maryland	1	Pennsylvania	6
Kentucky	1	New York	63	Vermont	21
Michigan	1	N. Hampshire	5	Virginia	2

YEARS OF ARRIVAL.

1818	1	1833	16	1837	20
1826	3	1834	15	1838	11
1831	4	1835	22	1839	12
1832	5	1836	40	Total	149

AGES.

50	1	61	3	72	1
51	2	62	6	73	2
52	1	63	8	74	2
53	3	64	19	75	4
54	4	65	10	76	7
55	3	66	14	77	3
56	2	67	7	78	1
57	6	68	6	79	1
58	5	69	6	80	2
59	7	70	6	81	0
60	5	71	1	82	1

APPENDIX.

RESPONSE FROM CHICAGO'S FIRST SCHOOL-TEACHER.

JOLIET, Ill., 22d June, 1879.

Messrs. Silas B. Cobb, Franklin D. Gray, Mark Kimball, Marcus C. Stearns, James N. Rees, Frederick Tuttle, and Joel C. Walker, Committee of Reception, Calumet Club.

GENTLEMEN:—If your invitation had reached me in time, the infirmities of age would have prevented my attendance. Nevertheless, I thank you for your kind remembrance. It certainly would have afforded me great pleasure to have embraced such a golden opportunity to meet old friends whom I can never expect to meet again on earth.

I arrived in Chicago in May, 1832, and have always had the reputation of being its first school-teacher. I never heard my claim disputed. I commenced teaching in the fall, after the Black-Hawk war, 1832. My first school-house was situated on the North-Side, about half-way between the lake and the forks of the river, then known as Wolf Point. The building belonged to Col. Richard J. Hamilton; was erected for a horse-stable, and had been used as such. It was twelve feet square. My benches and desks were made of old store boxes. The school was started by private subscription. Thirty scholars were subscribed for. But many subscribed who had no children. So it was a sort of free-school, there not being thirty children in town. During my first quarter I had but twelve scholars, and only four of them were white. The others were quarter, half, and three-quarter Indians. After the first quarter, I moved my school into a double log-house on the West-Side. It was owned by Rev. Jesse Walker, a Methodist minister, and was located near the bank of the river where the north and south branches meet. He resided in one end of the building, and I taught in the other. On Sundays, Father Walker preached in the room where I taught.

In the winter of 1832–3, Billy Caldwell, a half-breed

chief of the Pottawatomie Indians, better known as Sauganash, offered to pay the tuition and buy books for all Indian children, who would attend school, if they would dress like the Americans, and he would also pay for their clothes. But not a single one would accept the proposition conditioned upon the change of apparel.

When I first went to Chicago, there was but one frame building there, and it was a store owned by Robert A. Kinzie. The rest of the houses were made of logs. There were no bridges. The river was crossed by canoes.

I was born in Scipio, Cayuga County, New York, in 1802. I left Chicago in 1836, and have resided in Joliet and vicinity ever since. I had the acquaintance, when in Chicago, of Col. Richard J. Hamilton, Thomas Owen, (Indian Agent), George W. Dole, John Wright, P. F. W. Peck, Philo Carpenter, John S. C. Hogan, Col. John B. Beaubien, Mark Beaubien, John H., Robert A., and James Kinzie.

I will now give you the names of some of my scholars: Thomas, William. and George Owen; Richard Hamilton; Alexander, Philip, and Henry Beaubien; and Isaac N. Harmon, now a merchant in Chicago.

I remember Stephen R. Beggs, who sometimes preached in Father Walker's building where I taught school.

Respectfully yours,
JOHN WATKINS.

Response from Norman K. Towner.

YPSILANTI, *May 22, 1879.*

GENTLEMEN: I. am honored by the receipt of your kind invitation to meet the old settlers of Chicago at a reunion on the 27th.

I regret my inability to be with you on so memorable an occasion, and all the more when I see in the list of names represented so many, familiar in the early days, who, by daily toil, discharging daily duty, helped lay the foundation, hard and strong, of that magnificent superstructure which by the name of Chicago is known over two continents by those who have the ability to buy and the enterprise to cook good bread and good meat.

While glad to see so many yet left among the living, I cannot but note the absence of so many of their fellow-workers, like John B. Turner, George W. Dole, William B. Ogden, William H. Brown, Walter L. Newberry, John H. Kinzie,—"stalwarts" in the grand army of peace,—and others of lesser power or opportunity, who, a faithful day's work done, have laid them down to merited rest.

Pardon me for glancing at some of the first steps taken in securing the full benefits of Chicago's position at the head of lake navigation. How elated we were when on a certain Fourth of July the pioneer shovelful was thrown— and I am glad to see the vigorous arm that threw it still left among you (I refer to the Hon. Gurdon S. Hubbard)— that was to open the water-way across the prairies and enable old Father Michigan to reach over and join hands with Miss Sippi. Next the old Galena & Chicago Union Railroad, the first spoke in that now vast wheel of which Chicago is the hub, slowly but persistently stretched westward until it laid hold of the valley of Rock River and made itself felt as an added commercial channel. Then pantingly came the Michigan Central and Southern to shorten the Eastern way and make us independent through winter's cold as well as summer's heat. We had, too, some gala days; conspicuous that of the River and Harbor Convention, when our Fire Brigade was taxed to its utmost to aid the City make a decent demonstration in honor of its guests. But our little band had *Burley* firemen, two, at least, a *Bishop* to bless it, sound timber that for lack of better name we called *Underwood*, a *Gale* to blow it onward, and even a *Cobb* to "shell out" in its behalf.

We were not totally lacking for military glory. Under the lead of the gallant Hunter we charged down the line of the Illinois & Michigan Canal in bristling sleigh-loads, saw the rebellion, dispersed it, retired to our homes again while "the enemy" went to his shanty.

I am confident, gentlemen, you will so enjoy this present reunion as to be induced to hold frequent future ones. May you long live to do so. Yet, in the nature of things, it must be expected that another decade will thin your ranks, requiring those that may be left to stand the closer together.

Again thanking you most heartily for your kind invitation, I bid you good-by, invoking the blessing of the Supreme Ruler upon each and all. Most sincerely and truly your old friend, N. K. TOWNER.

Response from Rev. Flavel Bascom.

HINSDALE, Ill., May, 1879.

GENTLEMEN: I have received your card of invitation, and examined with peculiar interest the names of invited guests. Those names were once so familiar to me, and represent old-time friends so highly valued, it would afford me the greatest pleasure to enjoy the proposed social reunion. But, to my sincere regret, a previous engagement for that same evening, in another part of the State, makes my attendance at your reception impossible.

When I remember the relation of these early settlers to the building and rebuilding of Chicago; how much of its greatness is due to their enterprise and sagacity, it affords me much satisfaction to have known them, and to have my name recognized as entitled to a humble place among theirs. Wishing them a happy reunion now, and a still happier one in the hereafter, I remain yours, very truly,

F. BASCOM.

Response from Maj.-Gen. David Hunter.

DEAR GEN. SHERIDAN:—Many thanks, for the very kind manner in which you have conveyed to me the invitation of the gentlemen of THE CALUMET CLUB, to be present at their reception to the "old settlers of Chicago." I am very much tempted to accept, but my age and many infirmities admonish me, that it is too late for me to join in such a grand frolic; but how I should like to be with you.

More than half a century since, I first came to Chicago on horseback, from Saint Louis, stopping on the way at the log-cabins of the early settlers, and passing the last house at the mouth of Fox River. I was married in Chicago, having to send a soldier one hundred and sixty miles, on foot, to Peoria, for a license. The northern counties in the State had not then been organized, and were all attached to Peoria County. My dear wife is still alive, and in good health; and I can certify, a hundred times over, that Chicago is a first-rate place from which to get a good wife.

Be pleased to convey to the gentlemen of THE CALUMET CLUB my best regards and thanks for their kind invitation.

Very sincerely,

DAVID HUNTER.

WASHINGTON, D. C., May 24th, 1879.

Response from Judge Ebenezer Peck.

Messrs. S. B. Cobb and others, Committee on Invitations:
                                    CHICAGO, 24th May, 1879.

GENTLEMEN: I acknowledge the receipt of your invitation from The Calumet Club, to be present on the 27th instant, at a reception to be given to the old settlers of Chicago.

I am pleased to be recognized and remembered as one of those old settlers, and my eager desire is to be present at a place where I may meet so many of those with whom I was acquainted in by-gone days (when this now great city was only a very small town), and for whom I entertain much respect, and of whom I have many pleasant recollections; but unfortunately for me, my age and infirmities compel me to deny myself the great enjoyment I should receive could I be present at a meeting of pleasure like that proposed.

While you and your guests will be recounting and enjoying pleasant reminiscences, I shall be in my room lamenting that I am prevented by fate from enjoying them with you. Vanished years and early ties are not always pleasant concomitants. May the ever-ruling Power kindly, bless you all and keep you happy.

Sadly but thankfully yours, an old settler of 1835, offers his congratulations.
                                                    E. PECK.*

Response from Rev. Jeremiah Porter.

Messrs. S. B. Cobb, F. D. Gray, Mark Kimball, Etc., Committee The Calumet Club Reception:
                        FORT D. A. RUSSELL, Wy. T., May 24.

DEAR GENTLEMEN: Thanks for your kind invitation this hour received to meet the "Old Settlers of Chicago" on Tuesday evening next.

My distance, a thousand miles west of your wonderful City to which I went with United States troops forty-six years ago this month, and the cradle of its first infant church I then began to rock (two survivors of which, beside Mrs. Porter and myself, Mr. Philo Carpenter and Mrs. Charles Taylor, remain unto this day), must be my apology for not being with you to greet them and some others whose honored names I find among your invited, who saw with me the first 300 who then, and earlier, laid the foundations, *far out of sight*, like those of E. W. Blatchford's shot-tower—eternal foundations, on which a city, in less than half a century, has sprung, of more than half a million of people. To review with them and others who have been co-workers since in its intellectual, commercial, scientific, and Christian wonderful prosperity, would be an event of peculiar joy for a lifetime. But I must not trespass on your time. Living voices present with you will thrill your hearts with joy in this review, as they tell what God hath wrought for your Garden City, the Queen of the West, and yet the central city of the continent; and, perhaps, to be the *largest* before our children are as old as we now are. In conclusion, allow me to send, as a matter of interest for your reading at leisure, a sermon of Dr. Arthur Mitchell, now pastor of the church I organized, preached on the forty-fifth anniversary of that event. I am, gentlemen, very gratefully yours,

JEREMIAH PORTER,
Post-Chaplain, United States Army.

Brief letters of regret were also received from the following early residents:—

Berdel, Nicholas,		Englewood, Ill.
Bishop, James E.	(1836)	Denver, Col.
Black, Francis,	(1836)	Hampton, Ill.
Blasey, Barnhard,		Grant Park, Ill.
Boggs, Charles T.		Chicago.
Boyer, Valentine A.		Chicago.
Burley, Charles,		Exeter, N. H.
Chamberlain, Rev. J. S.	(May 20, '39)	Robin's Nest, Ill.
Clarke, John L.		Chicago.
Cleaver, Edward C.		Chicago.
Corrigan, William,	(Oct., 1836)	" (Died July 15 '79.
Davlin, John,	.	Waukegan, Ill.
Dewey, Dennis S.	(June 11, 1839)	Monticello.
Dickinson, Augustus,		Chicago.
Flood, P. F.	(June 20, 1835)	Chicago.
Haines, John C.	(1835)	Waukegan, Ill.
Lind, Sylvester,		Lake Forest, Ill.
Loomis, Henry,	(1836)	Burlington, Vt.
McClure, Josiah E.		Chicago.

Metz, Christopher,   (Oct., 1837) Chicago.
Morris, Buckner S.   Chicago.
Taylor, W. H.   Brookline, Mass.
Temple, Peter,   Lexington, Mo.
Turner, John,   (April, 1835) Ravenswood, Ill.
Vail, Walter,   Newburgh, New York.
Wadsworth, E. S.   (1836) Chicago.
Wright, Truman G.   Racine, Wis.

(From the *Chicago Tribune*, May 28, 1879.)

The spacious parlors of the Calumet Club were thronged last evening with the venerable, but, as a rule, hale and hearty, representatives of a former generation,—the men who came to Chicago when it was not Chicago, properly speaking, but a thriving young village at the head of Lake Michigan; the pioneers of civilization, in a word, the "old settlers" of Chicago, whose coming here dates prior to 1840. It was a collection unique in its character, and one whose like is seldom seen. The representatives of all the walks of life, the veterans in years and in experience, the silver-haired, and the less venerable on whose heads the frosts of age had as yet touched but lightly,—all were there, and every last one of them insisting that he was just as young in spirits, if not in years, as he was forty years ago. And, to tell the truth, the unchecked and unrestrained friskness of even some of the older heads was proof positive of the lingering existence of a very pardonable desire to be boys again, or, if not boys, at least very young or middle-aged men. There were those who had not met for years, —some had not looked into each other's faces for a quarter of a century,—and the result of such a coming together as that of last evening was the renewing of old and tried friendships, the fervid clasping of many a hand, the utterance of many a heartfelt "God bless you."

The idea of this most pleasant reunion dates from the last annual meeting of the Calumet Club, when a resolution was introduced by Mr. Joel C. Walter, and unanimously adopted, providing for the appointment of a committee to invite all the old settlers whose names and addresses were obtainable, to attend a reception given them by this young but progressive organization, representing Chicago's wealth and culture. Messrs. S. B. Cobb, Franklin D. Gray, Mark

Kimball, James H. Rees, Joel C. Walter, Marcus C. Stearns, and Frederick Tuttle were appointed as such committee, and immediately set about preparing for the success of the event which passed off so happily last evening. Some difficulty was experienced in securing a full list of the venerables whose advent here dates back prior to 1840, but if any were omitted—and they must have been very few—it was not from any lack of desire on the part of the Committee to do the full measure of their duty, but simply from the inherent difficulty of the task, increased by the absence of anything like a complete list of the veterans living in Chicago and vicinity. A number of the invited ones sent letters of regret at their inability to be present,—a regret which was shared equally by themselves and those who were so fortunate as to be able to attend.

The veteran guests of the Club began to arrive shortly after 7 o'clock, and an hour later, when the programme of speech-making was to have been taken up, the later arrivals were still pouring in, and the era of handshaking and of renewing old acquaintances, and of refreshing old memories seemed but to have commenced. The evening's exercises were accordingly deferred until something like half an hour later, and, apparently, to nobody's lasting regret, for the calling up of old reminiscences was something in which all could and did take part, and with a deal of zest, too, that revealed the pleasurable pride the veterans took in dipping into the past.

An effort was made to get a complete registry of the names of all the old settlers, but, owing to the crowd, the process of registering was accompanied with some considerable difficulty. In addition to this, a number of the guests were compelled to leave at a comparatively early hour, and before they could get an opportunity, so great was the pressure upon the space and the accommodations, to put down their names.   *   *   *   *   *

The gathering was called to order at 8:30, by Mr. S. B. Cobb, Chairman of the Committee on Reception,   *   *   *   *   *   and, the programme being completed, the Chairman further announced that the Old Settlers would adjourn from business to lunch.

And the old settlers didn't stay upon the order of their going, but repaired at once to the lunch-rooms adjoining.

In one of these a long table was set with a cold supper of sandwiches, salads, and ices, reinforced by the delicious concoction of the fragrant berry. Such as could not get within this room were served in the reading-room. The table in the main supper-room was rendered additionally attractive by a clever imitation in wood of Fort Dearborn, placed directly in the centre. Ample justice was done the collation, which was attractive to the eye as well as to the palate, and the veterans' organs of speech naturally became even more loosened than before as they put the cheer where it would do the most good. After supper, Mark Beaubien got out his fiddle, "rosined" the bow, got the venerable instrument in tune, and in less time than it takes to write it "Long John" Wentworth had a number of choice spirits under way to the accompaniment of the liveliest kind of dances. The veterans, ably assisted by some of the young men who were n't exactly following out Long John's advice with regard to keeping such hours as would result in a surplus of corn on their Cobb (no more were the veterans themselves), scampered around at an equally lively rate, and the fun was of the fast and furious, though innocent, kind that a lot of happy children might indulge in. In short, it was glorious, and the old fellows, as well as the young fellows—to whom it must have been a novelty—enjoyed it for all it was worth. The festivities were drawn out until some time after midnight, when the gathering broke up, amidst many repetitions of the unanimous verdict that the old settlers' reception had been an unqualified success,—one far beyond the most sanguine hopes of its promoters,—and amidst a general wish that the reception might not be the last of its kind.

(From the *Chicago Evening Journal*, May 28, 1879.)

It was a happy thought on the part of THE CALUMET CLUB to tender a reception to all known survivors of the Chicago of forty years ago. That Club is composed, for the most part, of young and middle-aged men of business, those upon whom now rest the burdens of commercial affairs. Their club-house, on the corner of Michigan Avenue and Eighteenth Street, is admirably fitted for such a purpose. Over half of the large number of invitations were accepted, and a delightful evening was spent in reminiscences of early days in Chicago, to say nothing of the pleasures of music, dancing, and a choice and well-laden table. The proceedings extended until a late hour, but no one showed signs of weariness. After the refreshments followed the best part of the feast. That delightful Apollo, Mark Beaubien, discoursed music familiar to the ears, and the heels, too, of the old settlers, and several old-fashioned dances were improvised, and about midnight the company dispersed, all agreeing that the occasion had been one of rare delight.

It is to be hoped that this reception will prove the first of a series.

NAMES

OF THE

Old Settlers of Chicago,

WHO CAME PRIOR TO 1840,

REGISTERED

AT

THE CALUMET CLUB OF CHICAGO.

NAMES OF OLD SETTLERS OF CHICAGO, REGISTERED AT THE CALUMET CLUB.

NAME.	DATE OF ARRIVAL.	BIRTHPLACE.	AGE.	PRESENT ADDRESS.
Adams, William H.	1837, Sept.	Westport, Conn.	64	Chicago.
Adsit, James M.	1838, April 2.	Spencertown, N.Y.	70	Chicago.
Arnold, Isaac N.	1836, Oct.	Hartwick, N.Y.	64	104 Pine Street, Chicago.
Batchelor, Ezra,	1837, June 4,	Paxton, Mass.	59	Milwaukee.
Bailey, Bennet,	1834, August,	Harford Co., Md.	68	Chicago.
Baker, Franklin,	1838, May,	Watertown, N.Y.	62	Chicago.
Baldwin, William A.	1836, June 13,	Austerlitz, Columbia Co., N.Y.	71	263½ Ill. Street, Chicago.
Balsley, John,	1839,	Pennsylvania.	66	Chicago.
Bates, John,	1832, May 20,	Fishkill, Duchess Co., N.Y.	76	Chicago.
Beaubien, Mark,	1826,	Detroit, Mich.	79	Newark, Kendall Co., Ill.
Beecher, Jerome,	1838, July 1,	Remsen, N.Y.	61	Chicago.
Beggs, Stephen R.	1831, June,	Rockingham Co., Va.	78	Plainfield, Ill.
Blake, S. Sanford,	1834, June 15,	Burlington, Vt.	63	Racine, Wis.
Blodgett, Henry W.	1837, June,	Mass.	57	Waukegan.
Boone, Levi D.	1836, May 31,	Lexington, Ky.	70	Chicago.
Botsford, Jabez K.	1833,	Connecticut.	66	Chicago.
Bowen, Erastus S.	1833,	New York.	64	Chicago.
Bradwell, James B.	1834, June,	England.	51	Chicago.
Bryan, Frederick A.	1836, October,	England.	59	Chicago.
Burley, Arthur G.	1835, May 11,	Exeter, N. H.	66	Chicago.
Burley, Augustus H.	1837, May 25,	Exeter, N. H.	60	Chicago.
Campbell, James,	1836, May,	Northumberland Co., Penn.	70	Chicago.

85

Name	Date	Origin	Age	Location
Carter, Thomas B.	1838, Sept.	New Jersey.	62	Chicago.
Carpenter, Abel E.	1833, June,	Savoy, Mass.	65	Aurora, Ill.
Carpenter, Philo,	1832,	Mass.	74	Chicago.
Caton, John Dean,	1833, June,	Orange Co., N.Y.	67	Ottawa, Ill.
Church, William L.	1836, May 16,	Lima, N.Y.	62	Kenwood, Ill.
Clarke, Henry W.	1838, June,	Watertown, N.Y.	64	Chicago.
Clarke, I. J.	1836,	Vermont.	51	Chicago.
Couch, James,	1836,	New York.	79	Chicago.
Clarke, Norman,	1835,	Vermont.	71	Racine, Wis.
Cobb, Silas B.	1833, May 29,	Montpelier, Vt.	67	Chicago.
Cleaver, Charles,	1833, Oct. 23,	London, England.	64	Chicago.
Cook, Isaac,	1834, February,	New Jersey.	76	St. Louis.
Densmore, Eleazer W.	1835, Sept.	Paris, N.Y.	58	Chicago.
DeWolf, Calvin,	1837, Oct. 31,	Luzerne Co., Penn.	64	Chicago.
Dodson, Christian B.	1833, August,	Burwick, Penn.	69	Geneva, Ill.
Doty, Theodorus,	1837,	New York.	77	Chicago.
Drummond, Thomas,	1835, May,	Bristol, Maine.	69	Winfield, Dupage Co., Ill.
Egan, Wiley M.	1836, Nov.	Ballston, N.Y.	52	Chicago.
Elliott, James F. D.	1838, May 30,	New York.	55	Mattoon, Ill.
Ellithorpe, Albert C.	1839, April 1,	St. Albans, Vt.	56	Chicago.
Fergus, Robert,	1839, July 1,	Glasgow, Scotland.	64	Chicago.
Follansbee, Charles,	1836, May 9,	Massachusetts.	68	Chicago.
Freeman, Robert,	1833,	Pennsylvania.	70	Napierville.
Freer, L. C. Paine,	1836, May,	Auburn, N.Y.	65	Chicago.

NAME.	DATE OF ARRIVAL.	BIRTHPLACE.	AGE.	PRESENT ADDRESS.
Gale, Abram,	1835, May 22,	Warwick, Mass.	82	Galewood.
Gale, Stephen F.	1835, May,	Exeter, N. H.	67	Chicago.
Gates, Philetus W.	1837, June,	Madison Co., N.Y.	62	Chicago.
Germain, George H.	1839,	New York.	63	Chicago.
Gilbert, Samuel H.	1836, June,	Bristol, England.	76	333 Walnut St., Chicago.
Goodrich, Grant,	1834,	New York.	67	Chicago.
Goodrich, T. W.	1832,	Benson, N.Y.	58	Milwaukee.
Graff, Peter,	1836, Sept. 10,	Albany, N.Y.	64	Chicago.
Granger, Elihu,	1836,	New Hampshire.	76	Kaneville.
Grannis,—Amos,	1836,	New York.	54	Chicago.
Grant, James,	1834, April 23,	Enfield, North Carolina.	66	Davenport, Iowa.
Gray, Franklin D.	1839, Sep.	Sharon, Conn.	61	Chicago.
Gray, George M.	1834, June,	Sherborn, N.Y.	60	Chicago.
Gray, John,	1837,	New York.	68	Jefferson.
Gray, Joseph H.	1836, July,	Boston, Mass.	67	Hyde Park.
Gray, William B. H.	1837, Sept.	Boston, Mass.	58	Chicago.
Hadduck, Edward H.	1833, May,	Salisbury, N.H.	68	Chicago.
Hall, Philip A.	1836, June 4,	New York.	60	Chicago.
Hamilton, Polemus D.	1834,	New York.	65	Chicago.
Hanchett, John L.	1835, June,	New York.	73	Chicago.
Harmon, Isaac N.	1833, Aug. 3,	Fredonia, N.Y.	52	Chicago.
Hawley, John S.	1837, May,	Ridgefield, Conn.	59	Aurora, Ill.
Hickling, William,	1835, March,	England.	65	Chicago.

Name	Date	Place of Birth	Age	Residence
Higgins, Van H.	1837,	New York.	58	Kenwood.
Hilliard, Lorin P.	1836, May,	Unadilla Forks, N.Y.	64	Chicago.
Hoard, Samuel,	1836, Oct. 13,	Westminster, Mass.	80	205 Morgan St., Chicago.
Holden, Charles N.	1837,	New York.	63	Chicago.
Horton, Dennison,	1836, August,	Conn.	63	Chicago.
Howe, Frederick A.	1834, July,	Buffalo, N.Y.	50	Chicago.
Huntington, Alonzo,	1835,	Vermont	70	Chicago.
Hoyne, Thomas,	1837, Sept. 1,	New York.	61	Chicago.
Hubbard, Gurdon S.	1818, Oct. 1,	Windsor, Vt	76	243 White St., Chicago.
Jones, Nathaniel A.	1838, Sept.	Rutland, Vt	77	Chicago.
Kehoe, Michael,	1839, May,	Ireland.	73	390 W. 12th St., Chicago.
Kennicott, Jonathan A.	1832, May,	Albion, N.Y.	55	Kenwood, Ill.
Kimball, Mark,	1839, Sept.	Genesee Co., N.Y.	58	Chicago.
Kimball, Martin N.	1836, Oct.	Saratoga, N.Y.	68	Chicago.
Kimball, Walter,	1833, Sept.	Rome, N.Y.	69	Chicago.
King, Tuthill,	1835, April,	New York.	75	Chicago.
Knickerbocker, H. W.	1833, Oct.	New York.	66	Naperville.
Lane, Elisha B.	1836,	N. H.	64	Chicago.
Lane, James	1836,	Ireland.	75	Chicago.
Lock, William,	1839,	Philadelphia.	66	Chicago.
Loomis, Horatio G.	1834, May 3,	Burlington, Vt	64	Naperville.
Manierre, Edward,	1835, Aug. 4,	New London, Conn.	66	Prairie Ave., Chicago.
Marshall, James A.	1832,	London, Eng.	70	Chicago.
McDaniels, Alexander,	1836, May 27,	Bath, N.Y.	64	Willmette.

NAME.	DATE OF ARRIVAL.	BIRTHPLACE.	AGE.	PRESENT ADDRESS.
Mills, John R.	1839,	Connecticut.	65	Chicago.
Milliken, Isaac L.	1837, June 17;	Saco, Maine.	63	Chicago.
Miltimore, Ira,	1836,	Vermont. [Died June 10, '79.]	66	Janesville, Wis.
Morrison, Daniel,	1835,	New York.	59	Chicago.
Morrison, Ephriam,	1834, Oct.	Oneida Co., N.Y.	64	Chicago.
Morrison, Ezekiel,	1833,	New York.	68	Chicago.
Murphey, James K.	1835, August,	Ireland.	54	Chicago.
Murray, R. N.	1831, July,	Washington Co., N.Y.	64	Naperville.
Myrick, Willard F.	1837, April,	Bridgeport, Vt.	69	Chicago.
Noble, John,	1831, June,	Yorkshire, Eng.	76	743 Sedgwick St., Chicago.
Ogden, Mahlon D.	1836, June 14,	Walton, Delaware Co., N.Y.	67	Elmhurst, Ill.
Oliver, John A.	1839, June,	Elizabeth, Union Co., N.J.	64	Chicago.
Osborn, A. L.	1835, July,	Watertown, Conn.	64	Laporte, Ind.
Osborn, William,	1834, May 1,	Ridgefield, Conn.	67	Chicago.
Page, Peter,	1837, June 12,	Pompey, N.Y.	64	Chicago.
Peacock, Joseph,	1836,	England.	66	Chicago.
Pierce, Asahel,	1833, Oct. 8,	East Calais, Wash. Co., Vt.	66	Chicago.
Pool, J. W.	1831, Oct.	Philadelphia.	75	149 W. Wash. St., Chicago.
Porter, Hilbard,	1833, Sept.	Jefferson Co., N.Y.	72	Chicago.[Died May 30, '79.
Powers, William G.	1835, May,	Auburn, N.Y.	65	Chicago.
Price, Cornelius,	1836, Sept.	New York City.	59	Chicago.
Prindiville, John,	1836,	Ireland.	54	Chicago.
Prindiville, Redmond,	1836, Aug. 23,	Ireland.	53	Chicago.

Raymond, Benj. W.	1836, June 5,	Rome, Oneida Co., N.Y.	77 Calumet Ave., Chicago.
Rees, James H.	1834, Aug. 11,	Stroudsburg, Penn.	66 Chicago.
Rexford, Stephen,	1833, June 27,	Charlotte, Vt.	75 Blue Island, Ill.
Richards, James J.	1835, July,	Salina, N.Y.	54 Evanston.
Rodgers, Edward K.	1835, Nov.	Ipswick, Mass.	66 359 Ontario St., Chicago.
Rumsey, George F.	1836, June 14,	Troy, N.Y.	59 Chicago.
Rumsey, Julien S.	1835, July 28,	Batavia, N.Y.	56 Chicago.
Satterlee, M. I..	1836,	Litchfield, Conn.	65 Chicago.
Sawyer, Sidney,	1839, May,	Albany, N.Y.	68 301 Ontario St., Chicago.
Scammon, J. Young,	1835, Sept.	Whitefield, Maine.	66 Hyde Park.
Scott, Willis,	1826,	New York.	69 Chicago.
Scott, Willard,	1826, Aug. 26,	New York.	71 Naperville.
Scoville, William H.	1837, May,	New York.	56 Chicago.
Sherman, Alanson S.	1836, Nov. 1,	Vermont.	68 Waukegan.
Sherman, Ezra I.	1836,	Newtown, Conn.	61 Riverside.
Sherman, Oren,	1836, Nov. 1,	Vermont.	63 15 E. Van Buren Street.
Skinner, Mark,	1836, July,	Manchester, Benn'gton Co., Vt.	65 Chicago.
Smith, David S.	1836, May,	Camden, N. J.	63 Chicago.
Snowhook, William B.	1836,	Ireland.	64 Chicago.
Sollitt, John,	1838,	York, England.	65 Chicago.
Stearns, Marcus C.	1836, Aug.	Naples, N.Y.	63 Chicago.
Steele, James W.	1836, Nov. 7,	New York.	71 Chicago.
Stewart, Hart L.	1832,	New York.	76 Chicago.
Stubbs, S. A.	1835,	State of New Jersey.	71 Chicago.

NAME.	DATE OF ARRIVAL.	BIRTHPLACE.	AGE.	PRESENT ADDRESS.
Sturtevant, Austin D.	1838, July,	Thetford, Vt.	63	Chicago.
Surdam, Samuel J.	1839, May,	Troy, N.Y.	62	Chicago.
Taylor, Edmund D.	1835, April,	Virginia.	76	Chicago.
Tripp, Robinson,	1834,	Vermont.	74	Chicago.
Tuttle, Frederick,	1836, Jan. 3,	New York.	70	Chicago.
VanNortwick, John,	1837,	New York.	70	Kane Co., Ill.
VanOsdel, John M.	1837, June 9,	Baltimore.	67	Chicago.
Wadhams, Seth,	1835, July 4,	Goshen, Conn.	66	Elmhurst, Ill.
Waite, George W.	1839, Nov. 15,	Walcott Village, N.Y.	60	Hyde Park.
Wolcott, Alexander,	1834, June 4,	Middletown, Conn.	64	Chicago.
Walter, Joel C.	1837, June,	Goshen, Conn.	68	Chicago.
Wentworth, John,	1836, Oct. 25,	Sandwich, N. H.	64	Chicago.
Whitehead, Henry,	1833, Sept.	Chatham, England.	68	Chicago.
Wilcox, Sextus N.	1839. Oct.	Stockbridge.	53	Chicago.
Willard, Alonzo J.	1838, Sept.	Lancaster, N. H.	62	Chicago.
Williams, Eli B.	1833, April,	Tolland, Conn.	80	Chicago.
Wilson, John L.	1834, May,	New York City.	65	Chicago.
Winship, James,	1836, Nov.	Palmyra, N.Y.	53	Chicago.
Yates, Horace H.	1838, March 14,	New York.	64	Chicago.

INDEX

TO

THE PROCEEDINGS OF THE FIRST "RECEPTION TO THE SETTLERS OF CHICAGO PRIOR TO 1840, [AS COMPILED BY HON. JOHN WENTWORTH], BY THE CALUMET CLUB, MAY 27, 1879."

[This Index was prepared by Mr. Wentworth, August, 1881.]

A.

Adams, Charles, 11.
Adams, John Quincy, 58.
Adams, Joseph, 11.
Adams, William H., 11, 51, 57, 84.
Adsit, James M., 11, 84.
Adsit, James M., jr., 5.
Aldrich, William, 5.
Alexander, G. M., 5.
Allen, Edward R., 11
Allen, Thomas, 11.
Allerton, Samuel W., 5.
Allison, Thomas, 11.
Anderson, T. W., 5.
Andrews, Joseph H., 5.
Angell, William A., 5.
Archer, William B., 53.
Areadne (vessel), 38.
Armour, George, 54.
Armour, George A., 5.
Armour, Joseph F., 5.
Arnold, Isaac N.; 11, 31, 50, 56, 57, 59, 84.
Asay, E. G., 5.
Asay, J. F., 5.
Ashwell, W. C., 5.
Averill, A. J., 5.
Ayers, Enos, 5.

B.

Bacon, Henry M., 5.
Bacon, Roswell B., 5.
Baker, William T., 5.
Baker, W. Vincent, 5.
Bailey, Amos, 11, 52.
Bailey, Bennett, 11, 84.
Balcom, Uri, 5.
Ballard, D. P., 5.
Baker, Franklin, 11, 84.
Baldwin, W. A., 11, 84.
Balestier, Joseph N., 11, 50, 84.
Balsley, John, 11, 84.
Barnes, Charles J., 5, 6, 9.
Barnes, R. B., 11.
Barrett, O. W., 6.
Bartlett, A. C., 6.
Bartlett, Charles S., 6.
Bascom, Flavel, 11, 52, 76.
Batchelor, Ezra, 12, 84.
Bates, John, 12, 36, 84.
Baumgarten, Chris, 12.
Baumgarten, John, 12.
Beach, James S., 12.
Beaubien, Alexander, 74.
Beaubien, Henry, 74.
Beaubien, John Baptiste, 35, 74.
Beaubien, Mark, 12, 31, 36, 37, 39, 40, 42, 43, 48, 49, 60, 61, 70, 71, 74, 81, 82, 84.
Beaubien, Medore B., 12, 49, 51, 74.
Beaubien, Philip, 74.
Beecher, Jerome, 12, 31, 58, 84.
Beggs, Stephen R., 12, 23, 24, 47, 74, 84.
Berdel, Nicholas, 12, 78.
Berg, Anton, 12.
Bigelow, A. A., 6.
Billings, Charles A., 6.
Billings, H. F., 6.

Birch, Hugh T., 6.
Bishop, Henry W., 6.
Bishop, James E., 12, 51, 75, 78.
Bismarck, *Prince*, 29.
Black, Francis, 12, 78.
Black Hawk (Indian chief), 50, 60.
Blackstone, T. B., 6.
Blackman, Edwin, 12, 51, 59.
Blair, Chauncey B., 6.
Blair, Chauncey J., 6.
Blair, Watson F. 5, 6.
Blake, *Capt.* Chelsey, 54.
Blake, E. Sanford, 12.
Blake, L. S., 12.
Blake, S. Sanford, 84.
Blasy, Barnhard, 12, 78.
Blatchford, E. W., 78.
Blodgett, Henry W., 12, 31, 43, 44, 57, 58, 59, 63, 84.
Boggs, Charles T., 78.
Bonaparte, Napoleon, 27.
Boone, Levi D., 12, 31, 51, 56, 57, 84.
Borland, J. J., 6.
Botsford, Jabez K., 12, 31, 51, 52, 84.
Botsford, Moss, 12.
Bowen, Erastus S., 12.
Boyer, Valentine A., 12, 49, 51, 78.
Bradley, Asa F., 12, 52.
Bradley, Timothy M., 12, 57.
Bradwell, James B., 12, 84.
Brainard, *Dr.* Daniel, 34.
Bridges, T. B., 12.
Briggs, Clinton, 6.
Brooks, Henry, 12.
Brooks, Joshua, 12.
Brooks, Samuel M., 12.
Bross, William, 70.
Brown, Andrew, 6.
Brown, Andrew J., 12, 51, 55.
Brown, Henry, 55.
Brown, Lemuel, 12.
Brown, J. M., 6.
Brown, Nathaniel J., 12, 60.
Brown, William H., 34, 75.
Bryan, Fred. A., 12, 84.
Bryant, J. Ogden, 6.
Buchanan, James, 59.
Buckingham, C., 6.
Burgess, Wm. T., 54.
Burley, Arthur G., 13, 31, 51, 58, 75, 84.
Burley, Augustus H., 13, 31, 57, 75, 84.

Burley, Charles, 13, 75, 78.
Burnham, D. H., 6.
Butler, John H., 13.
Butterfield, Justin, 34.
Byford, Henry T., 6.

C.

Cæsar, Augustus, 45.
Caldwell, Archibald, 13, 30, 47.
Caldwell, Billy (Indian chief), 48, 49, 73, 74.
Calhoun, Alvin, 34, 68, 69.
Calhoun, John, 34, 68.
Campbell, Augustus S., 6.
Campbell, B. H., jr., 6.
Campbell, James, 13, 84.
Canda, Florimond, 13.
Carpenter, Abel E., 13, 85.
Carpenter, Philo, 13, 31, 49, 50, 51, 59, 74, 77, 85.
Carroll, Edward, 13.
Carver, W. S., 6.
Carter, Thomas B., 13, 31, 51, 85.
Casey, Edward, 40, 70.
Cassidy, J. A., 6.
Caton, Arthur J., 6.
Caton, John Dean, 13, 31, 34, 35, 40, 47, 50, 51, 56, 58, 67, 69, 85.
Chacksfield, George, 13, 51, 85.
Chamberlain, *Rev.* J. S., 13, 78.
Chamblee (or Shabonee, Indian chief) 48.
Chapin, John P., 30, 66, 67, 69.
Che-che-pin-qua (or Alexander Robinson, Indian chief), 48.
Chisholm, William, 5, 6, 9.
Chumasero, John T., 6.
Church, William L., 13, 57, 85.
Clarissa (sloop), 54.
Clark, John K., 48.
Clark, John L., 13, 78.
Clark, John M., 6.
Clark, Stewart, 6.
Clark, T. B., 25.
Clarke, Abram F., 13.
Clarke, Henry B., 34.
Clarke, Henry W., 13, 51, 54, 85.
Clarke, L. J., 13, 85.
Clarke, Norman, 13, 85.
Clarke, Samuel C., 13.
Cleaveland, James O., 6.
Cleaver, Charles, 13, 52, 85.
Cleaver, Edward C., 13, 78.
Clybourn, Archibald, 34, 48.

INDEX.

Clybourn, Henly, 34, 48.
Clybourn, Jonas, 34, 48.
Cobb, Calvin, 6.
Cobb, Silas B., 6, 9, 11, 13, 23, 24, 25, 31, 34, 36, 52, 59, 60, 71, 73, 75, 77, 79, 80, 81, 85.
Coburn, Charles E., 6.
Coburn, Joseph G., 6.
Coburn, Lewis L., 6.
Collier, Z. Clinton, 6.
Collins, James H., 40.
Collins & Caton (firm), 40.
Comes, Charles W., 6.
Connell, Charles J., 6.
Cook, Isaac, 13, 51, 52, 57, 59, 85.
Cook, Thomas, 13.
Cooper, E. M., 6.
Corrigan, William, 13, 78.
Corwith, Gurden, 6.
Corwith, Henry, 6.
Corwith, Nathan, 6.
Couch, Ira, 34.
Couch, James, 13, 85.
Counselman, Charles, 6.
Cowles, Alfred, 6.
Cox, R. W., 6.
Crane, Albert, 6.
Crane, Charles A., 6.
Crerar, John, 6.
Critchell, R. S., 6.
Crocker, Hans, 13, 54.
Culbertson, C. M., jr., 6.
Curtiss, James, 34.

D.

Davidson, O., 13.
Davis, Jefferson, 53.
Davlin, John, 13, 57, 78.
Densmore, Eleazer W., 13, 58, 85.
Derby, W. M., 6.
Dewey, A. A., 6.
Dewey, Dennis S., 13, 78, 85.
DeWolf, Calvin, 13, 85.
Dexter, A. A., 13.
Dickey, Hugh T., 14, 31, 51, 54, 57, 58, 85.
Dickinson, Augustus, 14, 78.
Doane, J. W., 6.
Dodge, George E. P., 6.
Dodge, Martin, 14.
Dodge, Usual S., 14.
Dodson, Christian B., 14, 53, 85.
Dole, George W., 39, 74, 75.
Doty, Theodorus, 14, 85.

Douglas, Stephen A., 51.
Drake, John B., 6.
Drew, Charles W., 5, 6.,
Drummond, Thomas, 14, 31, 57, 58, 85.
Duck, Charles H., 14.
Dwight, J. H. 6.
Dyer, Charles V., 34.
Dyer, George R., 14.
Dyer, Thomas, 34.

E.

Eddy, Augustus N., 5, 6, 9.
Eddy, Devotion C., 51, 85.
Edgell, Stephen M., 14.
Egan, William B., 34.
Egan, Wiley M., 14, 85.
Eldridge, John W., 14, 31, 51.
Ellis, Joel, 14.
Elliot, James F. D., 14, 85.
Ellithorpe, Albert C., 14, 85.
Estes, Mrs. Elijah, 25.

F.

Fairbank, N. K., 6.
Fake, Henry, 14.
Fargo, Charles, 6.
Fauntleroy, T. S., 6.
Fergus, Robert, 14, 85.
Field, Marshall, 6.
Filer, Alanson, 14.
Filmore, Millard, 59.
Fisher, Fred P., 6.
Fleetwood, Charles, 6.
Fleetwood, Stanley, 6.
Fleming, Robert H,, 6.
Flood, Peter F., 14, 78.
Follansbee, Charles, 14, 31, 57, 85.
Foss, Robert H., 57.
Foster, John H., 30.
Freeman, Robert, 14, 85.
Freer, L. C. Paine, 14, 31, 85.
Fuller, George W., 6.
Fuller, William A., 6.
Fullerton, Alexander N., 14, 50.

G.

Gage, Albert S., 6.
Gage, Jared, 14.
Gage, John, 14, 56.
Gale, Abram, 14, 86.
Gale, Stephen F., 14, 31, 51, 52, 75, 86.

Gardner, C. S., 7.
Garrett, Augustus, 31, 34, 60, 66, 67, 69.
Garrett, Brown & Co. (firm), 60.
Gates, Philetus W., 14, 86.
Germaine, George H., 14, 86.
Getchell, E. F., 7.
Gilbert, Samuel H., 14, 86.
Glover, Samuel J., 7.
Goodhue, Josiah C., 66, 67, 69.
Goodman, James B., 5, 7.
Goodrich, Grant, 14, 31, 49, 50, 51, 52, 54, 56, 62, 70, 86.
Goodrich, Thomas Watson, 14, 86.
Goodwin, Jonathan, 7.
Goold, Nathaniel, 14.
Gore, George P., 7.
Gorton, Anson, 7.
Gould, M. B., 7.
Graff, Peter, 14, 86.
Granger, Elihu, 14, 57, 86.
Grannis, Amos, 15, 57, 86.
Grannis, S. W., 15.
Grannis, W. C. D., 7.
Grant, James, 15, 31, 44, 45, 51, 58, 86.
Grant, W. S., 59.
Graves, Henry, 15.
Graves, Dexter, 39.
Gray, Charles M., 15, 57.
Gray, Franklin D., 7, 9, 11, 15, 31, 73, 77, 79, 86.
Gray, George M., 15, 31, 86.
Gray, John, 15, 31, 57, 86.
Gray, Joseph H., 15, 31, 86.
Gray, William B. H., 15, 31, 86.
Green, Russell, 15.
Grey, William, L., 7.
Gurnee, Walter S., 15, 57.

H.

Hackett, John, 15.
Hackney, H. C., 7.
Hackney, John J., 7.
Hadduck, Edward H., 15, 39, 56, 59, 68, 86.
Haines, Elijah M., 15, 57.
Haines, John C., 15, 57, 78.
Hall, Amos T., 7.
Hall, Benjamin, 15, 47, 86.
Hall, David, 48.
Hall, Phillip A., 86.
Hall, William S., 7.
Hallam, *Rev.* Isaac W., 15, 34, 74.

Hamill, Charles D., 7.
Hamill, Ernest A., 7.
Hamilton, Polemus D., 15, 86.
Hamilton, Richard J., 30, 34, 73, 74.
Hanchett, John L., 15, 86.
Hanford, P. C., 7.
Hardin, S. H., 7.
Harmon, Elijah Dewey, 25, 34, 35.
Harmon, Isaac D., 15, 34.
Harmon, Isaac N., 15, 74, 86.
Harmon, Edwin R., 15.
Harrington Augustus M., 15.
Harrington, James C., 15.
Harrison, *Gen.* William H., 48, 59.
Haskell, Fred T., 7.
Hastings, Hiram, 15.
Hawley, John S., 15, 86.
Hayes, Rutherford B., 59.
Heacock, Russell E., 31, 34.
Heald, Hamilton, 15.
Heaton, E. S., 7.
Henderson, E. F., 7.
Henry, R. L., 7.
Hibbard, William G., 7
Hickling, William, 15, 86.
Higgins, Van H., 15, 31, 87.
Hilliard, Lorin P., 15, 87.
Hitchcock, *Rev.* Luke, 15, 52.
Hoard, Samuel, 15, 57, 59, 87.
Hodges, L., 7.
Hogan, John S. C., 34, 37, 74.
Holden, Charles N., 15, 59, 87.
Holbrook, John, 51.
Holliday, John M., 7.
Horton, Dennison, 15, 58, 87.
Howe, Fredrick A., 16, 87.
Hoyne, F. G., 7.
Hoyne, T. M., 7.
Hoyne, Thomas, 16, 31, 51, 56, 57, 58, 87.
Hubbard, Elijah K., 34.
Hubbard, Gurdon S., 16, 31, 37, 46, 51, 52, 53, 59, 64, 71, 75, 87.
Hubbard, Thomas H., 16.
Hughes, John B., 7.
Hugunin, James R., 16.
Hugunin, Lemuel C., 16.
Hull, *Gen.* William, 48, 71.
Humphreys, *Gen.* A. A., 16, 53.
Hunter, David, 16, 75, 76.
Hunter, George W., 16.
Huntington, Alonzo, 16, 51, 58, 87.
Huntoon, George M., 16.
Husted, H. H., 58.

Hutchings, Charles S., 7, 9.
Hyman, R. W., jr., 7.

I.

Isham, Henry P., 7.

J.

Jackson, Andrew, 47, 59.
Jackson, Carding, 58.
Jansen, E. L., 7.
Jefferson, Joseph, 55.
Jefferson, Thomas, 47.
Jenkins, T. R., 7.
Johnson, Andrew, 57, 59.
Johnston, William J., 7.
Jones, Fernando, 16.
Jones, Nathaniel A., 16, 87.
Jones, S. J., 7.
Jones, William, 31.
Judah, Noble B., 7.

K.

Keep, Albert, 7.
Keep, Chauncey, 7.
Keep, Fred A., 7.
Keep, Henry, 7.
Kehoe, Michael, 16, 87.
Keith, Edson, 5, 7.
Keith, O. R., 7.
Kelley, David, 7.
Kellogg, A. N., 7.
Kennicott, Jonathan A., 16, 87.
Kennicott, Joseph E., 16.
Kettlestrings, Joseph, 16.
Kimball, C. Fred, 7.
Kimball, C. P., 7.
Kimball, Harlow, 16.
Kimball, Mark, 7, 9, 11, 16, 31, 73, 77, 80, 87.
Kimball, Martin N., 16, 87.
Kimball, Walter, 16, 31, 51, 52, 53, 57, 59, 87.
Kimball, W. W., 7.
Kimbark, S D., 7.
King, Tuthill, 16, 31, 50, 51, 52, 87.
Kinzie, James, 34, 48, 74.
Kinzie, John, 47, 64.
Kinzie, John H., 30, 34, 64, 74, 75.
Kinzie, Robert A., 36, 64, 74.
Kinzie, William, 48.
Kirkpatrick, W. E., 7.
Knickerbocker, Abram V., 53.
Knickerbocker, Joshua C., 7.
Knickerbocker, H. W., 16, 87.

Knight, Darius, 16.
Knight, W. S., 7.
Kuhl, John, 16.

L.

Laflin, George H., 16.
Laflin, Mathew, 16, 31.
Lafromboise, Joseph, 49.
Lane, Elisha B., 16, 87.
Lane, George W., 16, 87.
Lane, James, 57, 87.
Larrabee, William M., 16, 56, 59.
Lathrop, Samuel, 16.
Law, Robert, 7.
Lay, A. Tracy, 7.
Leavenworth, Jesse H., 16, 53.
Leiter, Levi Z., 7.
Lester, John T., 7.
Lincoln, Abraham, 57, 59.
Lind, Sylvester, 16, 58, 78.
Lineburger, *Rev.* Isaac, 25.
Lock, William, 16, 58, 87.
Logan, John A., 7.
Loomis, Henry, 16, 78.
Loomis, Horatio G., 17, 51, 58, 87.
Loomis, John M., 7.
Loyd, Alexander, 34.
Ludington, Nelson, 7.

M.

Magill, Julian, 17.
Maher, Hugh, 17.
Marlborough, *Duke of*, 27.
Malony, Mathew S., 17.
Manierre, Edward, 17, 87.
Manierre, George, 34.
Markoe, Hartman, 17.
Marsh, Sylvester, 17.
Marshall, George E., 7.
Marshall, James A., 17, 58, 61, 87.
Martineau, Harriet, 29.
May, Edward, 7.
McCarthy, Owen, 17.
McClelland, H. W., 7.
McClure, Josiah E., 17, 78.
McDaniels, Alexander, 17, 87.
McDonnell, Charles, 17, 56.
McKee, David, 17, 47.
McIntosh, David, 17.
Meeker, George W., 68, 69.
Metz, Christopher, 17, 79.
Michigan (steamer), 54.
Miller, Jacob, 34, 48.
Miller, DeLaskie, 7.

Miller, John, 34, 48.
Miller, R. B., 7.
Miller, Samuel, 34, 48.
Milliken, Isaac L., 17, 57, 88.
Mills, John R., 17, 88.
Miltimore, Ira, 17, 56, 88.
Mitchell, Arthur, 78.
Mitchell, John J., 7.
Molony, Mathew S., 51.
Moore, Henry, 34, 58.
Moore, John, 54.
Moore, Robert, 17.
Morgan, Patrick R., 17.
Morley, E. W., 7.
Morris, Buckner S., 17, 31, 51, 56, 58, 70, 79.
Morrison, Daniel, 17, 88.
Morrison, Ephraim, 17, 88.
Morrison, Ezekiel, 17, 88.
Morse, T. E., 7.
Murphy, James K, 17, 88.
Murphy, John, 34.
Murray, Robert N., 17, 50, 54, 88.
Myrick, Willard F., 17, 88.

N.

Newberry, Walter L., 34, 55, 75.
Nichols, Luther, 17, 52.
Noble, John, 17, 88.
Norris, Joseph F., 58.
Norton, Nelson R., 17, 54.

O.

Oakley, J. W., 7.
Ogden, J. W., 7.
Ogden, Mahlon D., 17, 51, 57, 69, 88.
Ogden, William B., 34, 56, 69, 75.
Oliver, John A., 88.
Olmstead, Edward, 8.
Osborn, Andrew L., 17, 88.
Osborn, William, 17, 51, 88.
Otis, George L., 8.
Otis, Joseph E., 8.
Otis, Philo A., 8.
Otis, X. L., 8.
Owen, George, 74.
Owen, Thomas, 74.
Owen, Thomas J. V., 74.
Owen, William, 74.

P.

Packard, Edward A., 8.

Page, Peter, 17, 57, 88.
Page, William R., 8.
Pardee, Theron, 17.
Parker, John, 18.
Parker, Thomas L., 18.
Peacock, Elijah, 18.
Peacock, Charles D., 8.
Peacock, Joseph, 18, 88.
Peck, Clarence I., 8.
Peck, Ebenezer, 18, 77.
Peck, Ferdinand W., 8.
Peck, John L., 8.
Peck, Philip F. W., 34, 74.
Perry, Robert L., 5, 8.
Peters, George, 18.
Phelps, Erskine M., 8.
Pickering, Capt. ——, 38.
Pierce, Asahel, 18, 54, 56, 88.
Pierce, Franklin, 59.
Pierce, Smith D., 18.
Pitkin, Nathaniel, 18.
Plum, William B., 18.
Polk, James K., 59.
Pool, Capt. J. W., 18, 88.
Porter, Hibbard, 18, 88,
Porter, Rev. Jeremiah, 18, 52, 77, 78.
Porter, Mrs. Jeremiah, 77.
Porter, Rev. J. G., 18.
Powell, Samuel, 8.
Powers, William G., 88.
Price, Cornelius, 88.
Prindeville, John, 18, 88.
Prindeville, Redmond, 18, 88.
Pullman, George M., 8.

Q.

Quick, John H. S., 8.

R.

Ralston, R. W., 8.
Rand, Socrates, 18.
Raymond, Benjamin W., 18, 31, 51, 52, 56, 59, 89.
Rees, James H., 9, 11, 18, 31, 52, 73, 80, 89.
Reis, John M., 18.
Reis, Jacob, 18.
Reis, John P., 18.
Rexford, Norman, 18.
Rexford, Stephen, 18, 89.
Richards, James J., 18, 89.
Robinson, Alexander (or Che-che-pin-qua, Indian chief), 48.

INDEX.

Rockwell, A. L., 8.
Roe, John, 8.
Rogers, Edward K., 18, 51, 59, 89.
Rogers, John G., 8.
Root, J. S., 18.
Root, John W., 8.
Rue, John C., 18.
Rumsey, George F., 18, 31, 89.
Rumsey, Julien S., 18, 31, 57, 89.
Russell, Jacob, 34.
Russell, John B. F., 34.
Ryan, Edward G., 18.

S.

Saltonstall, F. G., 18.
Sare, William H., 8.
Satterlee, Merritt L., 18, 51, 89.
Sauganash (or Billy Caldwell, Indian chief), 48, 49, 74.
Sawyer, E. T., 8.
Sawyer, Nathaniel, 18.
Sawyer, Sidney, 18, 51, 89.
Scammon, J. Young, 19, 30, 31, 50, 57, 65, 68, 89.
Schneider, George, 8.
Scott, Willard, 19, 47, 89.
Scott, Willis, 19, 47, 50, 89.
Scott, *Gen.* Winfield, 50.
Scoville, William H., 19, 89.
See, *Rev.* William, 25.
Seeberger, A. F., 8.
Seeberger, C. D., 8.
Shabonee (or Chamblee, Indian chief), 48.
Shapley, Morgan L., 19, 53.
Shay, M. D., 8.
Shepard, J. H., 8.
Sheridan, *Gen.* Philip H., 8, 54, 76.
Sherman, Alanson S., 19, 52, 56, 58, 89.
Sherman, Ezra L., 19, 59, 89.
Sherman, Francis C., 34.
Sherman, Frank T., 19.
Sherman, J. S., 19.
Sherman, Oren, 19, 51, 89.
Shipman, Daniel B., 8.
Skeele, J. H., 8.
Skinner, Mark, 19, 31, 51, 57, 58, 59, 89.
Smith, Byron L., 8.
Smith, *Dr.* David S., 19, 51, 89.
Smith, Elijah, 19.
Smith, Fred I., 8.
Smith, George, 19.

Smith, Joseph F., 19.
Snowhook, William B., 19, 54, 57, 59, 89.
Sollett, John, 19, 89.
Soules, Rufus, 19.
Spaulding, S. F., 19.
Speer, Isaac, 19.
Spring, Giles, 34, 40.
Stager, Anson, 5, 8, 25.
Stanton, Daniel D., 19.
Stearns, Marcus C., 8, 9, 11, 19, 31, 73, 80, 89.
Steele, James W., 19, 89.
Stevens, George E., 8.
Stevens, Thomas H., 19.
Stewart, Hart L., 19, 31, 54, 57, 59, 89.
Stone, Joseph A., 8.
Stone, John, 58.
Stone, Lewis W., 19.
Storrs, Emory A., 8.
Stow, Henry M., 19.
Stow, William H., 19, 56.
Strail, J. Milo, 19, 51.
Strong, Henry, 8, 26, 34, 40.
Stubbs, S. A., 89.
Stuart, John T., 51.
Sturtevant, Austin D., 19, 90.
Surdam, Samuel J., 19, 51, 58, 90.
Sweeney, John, 19.
Sweet, *Mrs.* Charles, 25.
Swift, Richard K., 19.

T.

Talcott, Edward B., 19, 52, 53, 59.
Taylor, Augustine Deodat, 19, 31, 52.
Taylor, *Mrs.* Charles, 77.
Taylor, Edmund D., 20, 31, 46, 47, 51, 53, 57, 59, 90.
Taylor, Ezra, 20.
Taylor, Reuben, 20.
Taylor, William H., 20, 51, 52, 79.
Taylor, *Gen.* Zachary, 58, 59.
Tecumseh (Indian chief), 48, 49.
Temple, Peter, 20, 79.
Tenney, D. K., 8.
Thacher, J. M., 8.
Thompson, John L., 8.
Throop, Amos G., 57.
Toner, John, 20.
Towner, Norman K., 74, 75.
Tripp, Robinson, 20, 58, 90.
Tucker, W. F., jr., 8.

Turner, John, 20, 79.
Turner, John B., 34, 75.
Turner, John M., 20, 52.
Turner, Leighton, 20.
Tuttle, Frederick, 8, 9, 11, 20, 73, 80, 90.
Tuttle, Frederick B., 5, 8, 9.
Tuttle, Lucius G., 20.
Tyler, John, 57, 59.

U.

Underwood, John M., 20, 75.

V.

Vail, H. S., 8.
Vail, Walter, 20, 79, 90.
Vallette, Henry F., 20.
Van Buren, Martin, 51, 59.
Vandercook, Charles R., 20.
VanNortwick, John, 20, 90.
VanOsdell, John M., 20, 52, 90.
VanSchaack, Peter, 8.
VanSchaick, A. G., 5, 8, 9.

W.

Wadhams, Carlton, 20.
Wadhams, Seth, 20, 90.
Wadsworth, Elisha S., 20, 31, 51, 79.
Wadsworth, Julius, 20, 31, 56.
Waite, George W., 20, 90.
Walker, Rev. Jesse, 24, 48, 73, 74.
Walker, Lucy, 25.
Walker, Samuel B., 58.
Walker, William B., 8.
Walter, Joel C., 8, 9, 11, 20, 31, 51, 73, 79, 80, 90.
Walton, Nelson C., 20.
Warner, Seth P., 20.
Warner, Spencer, 20.
Warren, Julius M., 54, 60, 61, 63, 71.
Waters, Benjamin, 20.
Watkins, John, 20, 50, 74.
Watkins, Thomas, 49.
Watson, William, jr., 8.

Wattles, William W., 39.
Wellington, *Duke of*, 27.
Wells, M. D., 8.
Wentworth, Elijah, sr., 34.
Wentworth, Elijah, jr., 25, 34.
Wentworth, Moses J., 8.
Wentworth, John, 20, 31, 45, 71, 81, 90.
Wentworth, Lucy (Walker), 25.
Wetmore, C. L., 8.
Wheaton, George D., 8.
Wheeler, C. T., 8.
Wheeler, Ezra J., 8.
Wheeler, H. N., 8.
White, George, 36, 64.
Whitehead, *Rev.* Henry, 20, 90.
Whitney, J. C., 8.
Wicker, Charles G., 20.
Wicker, Joel H., 20.
Wight, Thomas, 8.
Wilbor, Philo A., 8.
Wilcox, Sextus N., 21, 90.
Wilde, George W., 21.
Williams, Abram, 8.
Williams, Clifford, 8.
Williams, Norman, 8.
Willard, Alonzo J., 21, 90.
Willard, Elisha W., 21.
Williams, Eli B., 21, 31, 51, 54, 56, 59, 90.
Williams, Giles, 21.
Wilson, Hugh R., 8.
Wilson, John L., 21, 34, 52, 57, 90.
Winship, James, 21, 90.
Wolcott, Alexander, 21, 52, 90.
Wood, Alonzo C., 21.
Woodruff, Charles W., 8.
Woodworth, James H., 34.
Woodworth, Robert P., 34.
Wright, George S., 21.
Wright, John, 31, 35, 74.
Wright, John S., 31.
Wright, Truman G., 21, 79.

Y.

Yates, Horace H., 21, 90.

www.ingramcontent.com/pod-product-compliance
Lightning Source LLC
Chambersburg PA
CBHW020858160426
43192CB00007B/984